*The Significance of Theory*

THE BUCKNELL LECTURES IN LITERARY THEORY
*General Editors: Michael Payne and Harold Schweizer*

The lectures in this series explore some of the fundamental changes in literary studies that have occurred during the past thirty years in response to new work in feminism, Marxism, psychoanalysis, and deconstruction. They assess the impact of these changes and examine specific texts in the light of this new work. Each volume in the series includes a critical assessment of the lecturer's own publications, an interview, and a comprehensive bibliography.

Frank Kermode        *Poetry, Narrative, History*
Terry Eagleton       *The Significance of Theory*
Toril Moi           *Feminist Theory and Simone de Beauvoir*

# The
# Significance
# of Theory

## Terry Eagleton

Basil Blackwell

First published 1990

Basil Blackwell Ltd
108 Cowley Road, Oxford, OX4 1JF, UK

Basil Blackwell, Inc.
3 Cambridge Center
Cambridge, Massachusetts 02142, USA

*British Library Cataloguing in Publication Data*

A CIP catalogue record for this book is available from the British
Library.

*Library of Congress Cataloging in Publication Data*

Eagleton, Terry, 1943–
     The significance of theory/Terry Eagleton.
        p. cm. — (The Bucknell lectures in literary theory)
     Includes bibliographical references.
     ISBN 0–631–17269–6 — ISBN 0–631–17271–8 (pbk.)
        1. Criticism—History—20th century. 2. Literature—History and
     criticism—Theory, etc. 3. Politics and literature. I. Title.
II. Series.
     PN94.E23 1989                                                    89–38730
     801'.95—dc20                                                          CIP

Typeset in 11 on 13 pt Plantin
by Photographics, Honiton, Devon
Printed in Great Britain by Billing & Sons Ltd, Worcester

# Contents

# Preface

Fundamental and far-reaching changes in literary studies, often compared to paradigmatic shifts in the sciences, have been taking place during the last thirty years. These changes have included enlarging the literary canon not only to include novels, poems and plays by writers whose race, gender or nationality had marginalized their work, but also to include texts by philosophers, psychoanalysts, historians, anthropologists, social and religious thinkers, who previously were studied by critics merely as 'background'. The stance of the critic and student of literature is also now more in question than ever before. In 1951 it was possible for Cleanth Brooks to declare with confidence that the critic's job was to describe and evaluate literary objects, implying the relevance for criticism of the model of scientific objectivity while leaving unasked questions concerning significant issues in scientific theory, such as complementarity, indeterminacy and the use of metaphor. Now the possibility of value-free scepticism is itself in doubt as many feminist, Marxist and psychoanalytic theorists have stressed the inescapability of ideology and the consequent obligation of teachers and students of literature to declare their political, axiological and aesthetic positions in order to make those positions conscious and available for examination. Such expansion and deepening of literary studies has, for many critics, revitalized their field.

Those for whom the theoretical revolution has been regenerative would readily echo, and apply to criticism, Lacan's call to revitalize psychoanalysis: 'I consider it to be an urgent task to disengage from concepts that are being deadened by routine use the meaning that they regain both from a re-examination of their history and from a reflexion on their subjective foundations. That, no doubt, is the teacher's prime function.'

Many practising writers and teachers of literature, however, see recent developments in literary theory as dangerous and anti-humanistic. They would insist that displacement of the centrality of the word, claims for the 'death of the author', emphasis upon gaps and incapacities in language, and indiscriminate opening of the canon threaten to marginalize literature itself. In this view the advance of theory is possible only because of literature's retreat in the face of aggressive moves by Marxism, feminism, deconstruction and psychoanalysis. Furthermore, at a time of militant conservativism and the dominance of corporate values in America and Western Europe, literary theory threatens to diminish further the declining audience for literature and criticism. Theoretical books are difficult to read; they usually assume that their readers possess knowledge that few have who have received a traditional literary education; they often require massive reassessments of language, meaning and the world; they seem to draw their life from suspect branches of other disciplines: professional philosophers usually avoid Derrida; psychoanalysts dismiss Freud as unscientific; Lacan was excommunicated even by the International Psycho–Analytical Association.

The volumes in this series record part of the attempt at Bucknell University to sustain conversation about changes in literary studies, the impact of those changes on literary art and the significance of literary theory for the humanities and human sciences. A generous grant from the Andrew W. Mellon Foundation has made possible a five-year series of visiting lectureships by internationally known participants in the reshaping of literary studies. Each volume includes a comprehensive introduction to the published work of the lecturer, the two Bucknell Lectures, an interview and a comprehensive bibliography.

# Introduction

At whatever level it is undertaken, the practice of literary criticism inevitably leads to questions of theory. In the midst of a class discussion students will ask earnestly, 'But could the author possibly have intended all we say he meant?' And in the midst of preparing a lecture or writing an article – possibly after having torn themselves away from a family event or news of the latest world crisis – critics will ask themselves with equal intensity, 'What is the point of this work I do? Does it relate intrinsically to anything that is genuinely important in my life or in the world at large?' Until fairly recently such questions only rarely got the attention they deserved, and then usually by philosophers rather than by critics or teachers of literature. Indeed, the avoidance of such questions has been actively encouraged by practitioners of American New Criticism. In his essay 'The Idealism of American Criticism', Terry Eagleton describes the New Criticism's strategic avoidance of theory in this way:

> Offspring of the failed agrarian politics of the 1930s, and aided by the collapse of a Stalinized Marxist criticism, New Criticism yoked the 'practical critical' techniques of I. A. Richards and F. R. Leavis to the re-invention of the 'aesthetic life' of the old South in the delicate textures of

the poem. . . . But since a mere Romanticism was no longer ideologically plausible, New Criticism couched its nostalgic anti-scientism in toughly 'objectivist' terms: the poem had the gemlike hardness of an 'urn' or 'icon', a structure of complex tensions cut loose from the flux of history and authorial intention, autotelic and unparaphrasable. . . . In response to the reification of society, New Criticism triumphantly reified the poem. (*AG*, p. 49)

Despite its powerful advantage of being immanently teachable, the New Criticism has proven to be intellectually and politically sterile to those who think that literature is not separable from life but participates instead in an unbreakable whole of what we know and do, as well as what we write. In the view of such critics as Eagleton, the student is right to want to be able to see a connection between what Milton wrote and how he lived; and critics are likewise right in wanting their own work to engage the complete range of their intellectual and political commitments.

Although his first book, *Shakespeare and Society* (1967), already showed an inclination toward criticism that engages not only literary texts but also the social movements that shape what the poet and the critic write, Eagleton's work since the mid-1970s has become more sharply focused in its politics. As he suggests in the preface to his recent collection of essays, *Against the Grain* (1986), his work can be roughly divided into two phases. The first phase reaches its climax in 1976 with *Criticism and Ideology* and *Marxism and Literary Criticism* and is powerfully influenced by the vitality of Marxist cultural theory in Britain and the rest of Europe that was inspired in turn by the now mythical 1960s: Vietnam, civil rights movements, student protests and university reform, development of the women's movement, events in Northern Ireland, and achievements of the labour movement – all generating the hope that fundamental social change was about to occur. The work of Louis Althusser was a particularly important influence on Eagleton during this period. The key to understanding Althusser's impact, Eagleton argues (*LT*, pp. 171–3) is the essay 'Ideology and Ideological State Apparatuses' in Althusser's *Lenin and Philosophy* (1971). In that essay Althusser proposes to explain how, even when the ruling class is working against their self-interests, people submit themselves to their society's ruling ideologies. Taking his cue from the psychoanalytic theory of Lacan, Althusser would account for the hold of ideology by such reflections as these: I can think of myself as a free, self-determined individual. I operate under the illusion of this freedom because of the impact of an ideology that all the while has me in its grip. In fact I am a mere function of a social structure that would operate perfectly well without me. I do not usually feel this way about my relationship to society, rather quite the opposite. 'I come to feel', Eagleton explains, 'not exactly as though the world exists for me alone, but as though it is significantly "centered" on me, and I in turn am significantly "centered" on it' (*LT*, p. 172). My combined sense of personal freedom and social purpose derive from the signs and social practices that bind me to the social structure, though in fact I am not in the least indispensible to it. I dress in a certain way; I listen to classical music and read the *New York Review*; I teach, write articles, go to committee meetings; I attend conferences and deliver papers. All of these activities bind me to the social orders that I am serving – the community in which I live, my university, America – by supplying me with a reasonably satisfying and unified image of myself: a middle-aged professor who may not be as well paid as he would like but who has the freedom to say what he thinks and to teach the books he loves to young people who are usually pleasant enough to be around and who attend classes on a campus that combines the comforts of modern life with the imaginary setting of the pastoral world. In fact, this ideology in which I participate, Eagleton argues via Althusser via Lacan, requires '*mis*-recognition' of me; it requires me to believe in the idealized image it offers me of my autonomous self. All of my social actions, all that I read and all that I write constitute the inescapable web of this ideology, which is in truth the Other but which I come to believe is myself. Despite its many flaws, Althusserian Marxism serves, Eagleton trenchantly observes, to confirm 'intellectuals in their professional status, while setting them violently – and so sometimes consolingly – at odds with the governing humanistic ideologies of their institutions' (*AG*, p. 2). It provides a way to live with one's own bad faith.

The second phase of Eagleton's work, which includes his study of Walter Benjamin, *The Rape of Clarissa*, *Literary Theory: An Introduction* and *The Function of Criticism*, confronts some of the limitations of Althusserianism, especially its similarity to nihilistic modes of existentialism in seeming to justify complete political inactivity in the face of the conservativism of the late 1970s and 1980s. Just as Althusser was an inspiring presence during the first phase, Benjamin's spirit presides over the more recent phase of Eagleton's work. In Benjamin's life and thought Eagleton discovers the encounter between Marxism and deconstruction (*WB*, p. 131). Eagleton sees both Marxism and deconstruction as acknowledging the ubiquity of ideology but as offering fundamentally different ways of dealing with it. That difference may be initially understood in terms of the deadlock between decisions to work inside or outside the capitalist system. Eagleton describes how this inside–outside distinction is very much alive in political practice, however suspect it may be in political theory:

> Social democracy believes in working on the 'inside' of the capitalist system: persuaded of its omnipotent, all-pervasive, as it were 'metaphysical' presence, it seeks nonetheless in

humble fashion to locate and prise open those symptomatic points of 'hesitancy', negativity and incompletion within the system into which the thin end of a slim-looking reformist wedge may be inserted. The forms of political theory and practice known to Marxism as 'ultra-leftism', by contrast, will have no truck with this feeble complicity. Equally convinced of the monolithic substance of the system as a whole, they dream, like the anarchist professor of Conrad's *The Secret Agent*, of some unutterable radical enterprise which would blow a black hole in the whole set-up and forcibly induce its self transcendence into some condition beyond all current discourse. (*WB*, p. 132)

The liberal social-democrat would press for more freedom of speech in Eastern Europe, while the radical ultra-leftist would attempt to achieve a workers' revolution.

This binary opposition between inside and outside is but an initial move in coming to terms with the meeting of Marxism and deconstruction. Indeed, the principal contribution of Althusserian ideology was the collapsing of that distinction: my sense of self is not *mine* but the ideal image of myself that ideology (language and social gesture) has manoeuvred me to accept as myself. The inside–outside opposition had already broken down in traditional Marxist thought once the working class was seen as the agent of historical revolution. Located within the capitalist mode of production by capitalism itself, the working class was both the sustaining force of capitalism and the means of its destruction. As Eagleton dramatically puts it: 'Capitalism gives birth to its own gravedigger, nurturing the acolyte who will one day stab the high priest in the back' (*WB*, p. 133). But like other millennialist visions, this one has not been realized in historical time and, by the failure of its realization, has created the several Marxisms and deconstructions of contemporary theory. This situation in which history holds its breath has parallels in the delayed messianic age in Judaism, as described by Benjamin's friend Gershom Scholem and in the false expectation of a new sense of historical time following the French Revolution, as described by George Steiner.

Just as Marxism now includes a spectrum of political practice ranging from democratic socialism to ultra-leftism, so deconstruction has its modest and radical extremes. As Eagleton puts it:

> Deconstruction is in one sense an extraordinarily modest proposal: a sort of patient, probing reformism of the text, which is not, so to speak, to be confronted over the barricades but cunningly waylaid in the corridors and suavely chivvied into revealing its ideological hand. Stoically convinced of the unbreakable grip of the metaphysical closure, the deconstructionist, like any responsible trade union bureaucrat confronting management, must settle for that and negotiate what he or she can within the left-overs and stray contingencies casually unabsorbed by the textual power system. But to say no more than this is to do deconstruction a severe injustice. For it ignores that other face of deconstruction which is its hair-raising *radicalism* – the nerve and daring with which it knocks the stuffing out of every smug concept and leaves the well-groomed text shamefully dishevelled. It ignores, in short, the *madness* and violence of deconstruction, its scandalous urge to think the unthinkable, the flamboyance with which it poses itself on the very brink of meaning and dances there, pounding away at the crumbling cliff-edge beneath its feet and prepared to fall with it into the sea of unlimited semiosis or schizophrenia. (*WB*, p. 134).

In its modest form deconstruction seeks out breaks, slippages, contradictions, vertiginous moments within the ideological discourses by which we are constituted; in its more radical form it promotes the dissolution of meaning in order to bring down the power structure of texts. The various modes of contemporary Marxism and deconstruction are for Eagleton more than strategies to deal with the failed or delayed hope of revolution. Deconstruction is the restless consciousness that refuses to be stilled by ideology, and Marxism is the active resistance to alienation and futility that spring from the class structures sustained by ideology.

Several features of Eagleton's work have helped to make him the most read theorist in Britain today. Not only does he write extremely well, he has also forged for himself a style that is neither mannered and arcane, nor detached and uncommitted. When he acts as a medium for some of the more elusive spirits of modern theory – as he does in *Marxism and Literary Criticism*, *Literary Theory: An Introduction* and his book on Benjamin – Eagleton is a model teacher. Clear and challenging, serious and witty, he invites us, as Benjamin did also, to confront the social and theoretical challenges of modern life without abandoning tradition. More than any other contemporary theorist since Northrop Frye and Frank Kermode, Eagleton moves easily among the major writers of the past – Shakespeare, Milton, Richardson, Johnson, the Brontes, Brecht – prodding his reader to reconsider their works and to question what he says about them. Because it subjects itself to the same dialectic by which it examines historical processes, Marxist cultural theory has, in Eagleton's view, a comic shape:

For Marxism, history moves under the very sign of irony: there is something darkly comic about the fact that the bourgeoisie are their own grave-diggers, just as there is an incongruous humour abut the fact that the wretched of the earth should come to power. The only reason for being a Marxist is to get to the point where you can stop being one. It is in that glib, feeble piece of wit that much of the Marxist project is surely summarized. Marxism has the

humour of dialectics because it reckons itself into the
historical equations it writes. (*WB*, p. 161)

Eagleton's criticism, too, has that same inviting shape of
comedy. In what is perhaps his most accessible book, *The
Function of Criticism*, Eagleton's critical mythos is clearest.
The argument of that book is that modern criticism has
lost its social function and has thus betrayed its heritage.
'Born of a struggle against the absolutist state' in the
seventeenth and eighteenth centuries, criticism became for
the European bourgeoisie a discursive space between
state and civil society in which 'rational judgement and
enlightened critique' broke free of authoritarian politics
(*FC*, p. 9). In that bourgeois public sphere of clubs,
journals and coffee-houses the rules of discourse were, as
Dryden describes them, 'founded upon good sense, and
sound reason, rather than on authority'. By narrowing the
focus of literature to an exclusive preoccupation with
canonical texts, criticism has undermined itself. 'It is
arguable', Eagleton writes, 'that criticism was only ever
significant when it engaged with more than literary
issues – when, for whatever historical reason, the "literary"
was suddenly foregrounded as the medium of vital concerns
deeply rooted in the general intellectual, cultural and
political life of an epoch' (*FC*, p. 107). Eagleton's project
is to recover criticism's traditional social role.

Like the final scene of a Shakespearean comedy, his
vision of criticism's reformation encompasses the diverse
occupations that now somewhat uneasily coexist under the
umbrella of English literature: 'semiotics, psychoanalysis,
film studies, cultural theory, the representation of gender,
popular writing, and of course the conventionally valued
writings of the past' (*FC*, p. 124). These various pursuits
are unified, as he sees them, only by 'a concern with the
symbolic processes of social life, and the social production
of forms of subjectivity' (*FC*, p. 124). Now more than

ever, Eagleton insists, we need in America and Europe 'a more profound understanding of such symbolic processes, through which political power is deployed, reinforced, resisted, at times subverted' (*FC*, p. 124) in order to be able to end power-struggles that threaten survival itself. Although he begins *The Future of Criticism* by confessing his intention 'flexibly and opportunistically, to shed light on a particular history' (*FC*, p. 8), Eagleton's flexibility is an ecumenical openness to the diversity of literary study today and his opportunism amounts to a concerned focus of attention on the contemporary occasion for criticism's recovery of its traditional role.

**Michael Payne**

Terry Eagleton's contribution to Marxist cultural theory is striking in its range. While his earlier writing examined in some depth certain Marxist categories of literary-cultural analysis, his later, more popularising, work has argued persuasively the need for theory. Eagleton has re-evaluated the English literary critical tradition, redefined the critic's function and reappraised specific authors from his historical materialistic perspective. These are substantive aspects of the general task of a Marxist critic. But what stands out more saliently in Eagleton's recent texts is his resolute critical engagement with and historical contextualization of, other modern critical trends. This aspect of Eagleton's work yields the vexed question that will be addressed here, namely what exactly is the relationship of Eagleton's Marxism to recent non-Marxist critical theory?

Eagleton has been criticized for being uncritically dismissive of post-structuralism; and, on the other side, for 'compromising' his Marxism. As Eagleton phrases it in the interview reproduced here, 'if one sits on a fence, that's when one draws fire from both sides'. But fences, particularly in Oxford, can be too sharp to sit on. And Eagleton's position, it will be argued here, entails not compromise but a strategism which is quite compatible with his Marxism.

From one point of view, virtually all modern literary theories, each with its own inflections and motives, can be regarded as an implicit if not direct reaction against the New Critical claims as to the autonomy, independence and objectivity of a literary text. Eagleton, as we shall see, has an ambivalent stance towards what he calls the 'radical anti-objectivism' of recent theory (*FC*, p. 93). What this reaction against objectivity entails, at a deeper level, is an assault on the notion of identity. It is perhaps at this level that one can see most clearly the nature of overlap and divergence between Eagleton's Marxism and non-Marxist theory.

In traditional logic, as deriving from its comprehensive formulation by Aristotle, the law of identity serves among other things as a basis of categorization and exclusive definition: an entity is what it is precisely because it is not anything else. Its identity is thus born in the process of dirempting its relations with other similarly 'identified' things in the world, a process which thereby denies ontical status to those relations, treating them as somehow external to the entities related. This suppression of relations and relegation of them to a contingent status, a procedure closely tied to Aristotle's various definitions of 'substance' and 'essence', can serve a political and ideological function. For example, the identity of an object (which could be simply a physical entity or something as complex as a system of law or religion) which is in fact historically specific could be passed off as an eternal or natural identity. As Eagleton remarks in his essay on Adorno in this volume, the notion of identity is 'coercive': it is the 'ideological element of pure thought' and was 'installed at the heart of Enlightenment reason'. It is installed also, one can infer, in all philosophies which positivistically accept the apparent given-ness of an object at face value, failing to see the object as essentially the result of a process whether philosophical or political.

The form of thought which most comprehensively impugns the notion of identity is dialectical thought. Hegel's *Logic* is explicitly an attack, conducted on a far higher level than its derivatives in Derrida's work, on the one-sidedness of traditional logic which fails to see identity as an intrinsic function of difference. It should be said that Eagleton has never sympathized with Hegelian Marxism, an antipathy partly taken over from Althusser. In *Criticism and Ideology* Eagleton was influenced (though by no means uncritically) by Althusser particularly with regard to the epistemological break between the earlier 'humanistic' and later 'scientific' attitudes which Althusser claimed to have found in Marx's work: it had been Althusser's intention to divest Marxism of Hegelian notions. But, quite apart from the facts that Eagleton has moved beyond Althusser's influence and has more recently acknowledged the lasting value of Lukács (whom he calls the greatest Marxist aesthetician, *WB*, p. 84), it should equally be observed that Eagleton has never denied the dialectical character of Marxism.

Marx, in both his earlier and later work, takes over some central features of the *form* of Hegel's dialectic: firstly, an imperative to abolish or negate the given object (or state of affairs) by articulating the full rationality of that object's relations with a particular social and historical context, showing how these relations constitute the object. That is why, when the bourgeoisie was the revolutionary class, the Hegelian system was called a 'negative' philosophy; it could be interpreted as revolutionary. In his 1844 manuscripts, Marx saw the 'outstanding achievement' of Hegel's *Phenomenology* as the recogntion of the 'dialectic of negativity' as the moving principle of history. And of course, as late as the famous preface to *Capital*, Marx still claimed adherence to the form, though not the idealist content, of Hegel's dialectic. Writing in 1859, Engels was at great pains to stress that the superiority of Hegel's thought to previous philosophy lay in 'the tremendous historical sense' of the dialectic. Engels goes on:

> Marx was and is the only one who could undertake the work of extracting from the Hegelian logic the kernel containing Hegel's real discoveries in this field, and of establishing the dialectical method, divested of its idealistic wrappings, in the simple shape in which it becomes the only correct form of developmental thinking. We consider the working out of the method which underlies Marx's critique of political economy a result of hardly less importance than the basic materialist conception. (*CPE*, p.55)

The second dialectical feature is a tendency to view an entity as unstable and intrinsically in a state of transition, being part of a more comprehensive process leading beyond it. This was an aspect of Hegel's ontological vision whereby, for example, 'existence' itself was viewed as contradictory. For Marx the notion of 'contradiction' acquires a social content, characterizing not only the historical relations between classes but also the central bourgeois concepts. The bourgeois notion of the 'individual', for instance, entails a contradiction between the individual's 'human' needs as a member of civil society and that individual's abstract identity as a 'citizen' of the state. The third aspect of the dialectic is the notion of 'sublation', which refers to the dual process of negating and transcending a given opposition or state of affairs while retaining certain features of what is negated. The extent to which this informs, for example, Marx's view of Communist society as arising out of bourgeois relations of production is problematic, not least in the realm of superstructure. According to Marx, a change in the 'economic foundation' is followed by more or less prolonged struggle in the ideological sphere (*CPE*, p. 4). The point is that one ideology or social structure does not simply replace another in linear fashion; whatever predominance is achieved is preceded by struggle and conflict. But even here it is a question of emphasis. Eagleton has little sympathy with Lukács's view of Marxist society which Eagleton characterizes as 'the triumphant sublation of the bourgeois humanist heritage' (*WB*, p. 83). But Eagleton acknowledges that 'Socialists . . . wish to draw the full, concrete, practical applications of the abstract notions of freedom and democracy to which liberal humanism subscribes' (*LT*, p. 208).

All three features of Hegel's dialectic, utilized by Marx and Engels, constitute an attack on the notion of simple identity. The dialectic moves through three stages. Initially an object is viewed in its given particularity as self-identical. In the second stage the object's 'identity' is viewed as externalized or dispersed through the totality of its social and historical relations: it is viewed in its universal aspect. In the third stage the object's identity is viewed as mediated (rather than immediately given) and as a combination of universal and particular. Marx adapted two other aspects of this process: the 'externalization' that was initially for Hegel an ontological notion, acquires political resonance for Marx as 'alienation'. And Hegel was right, according to Marx, in recognizing (albeit abstractly) that the so-called 'objective world' was in fact a product of subjective labour.

Eagleton affirms that the 'power of the negative . . . constitutes an essential moment of Marxism' (*WB*, p. 142). This perhaps gives us the clearest perspective from which we can understand how, in Eagleton's eyes, non-Marxist literary theory can be useful to Marxism. For there is a sense in which modern literary theories can be viewed as embodying 'negative' philosophies, attacking received notions of identity, subjectivity, objectivity and language. Non-Marxist theories effectively arrest the Hegelian dialectic at its second phase (of externalization and relationality) and their political valencies depend on the direction of their reintegration of that externality. For example, structuralism uses 'structure' and 'language' as a basis of reintegration. Psychoanalysis posits the 'unconscious', while deconstruction effectively posits 'difference'. Feminism and socialism use political goals as a basis. Eagleton brings out this 'negative' aspect of literary theory in some detail. Among the 'gains' of structuralism he ranks its demystification of literature, which it views not as a unique or essential discourse but as a construct. The codes of structuralism are indifferent to traditional compartmentalisations. Again, structuralism regards 'meaning' not as substantively self-identical but as relational, the product of a shared system of signification. Eagleton acknowledges that these views harbour an implicit 'ideological threat' to bourgeois representational and empiricist views of language and literature inasmuch as structuralism shows reality and experience to be discontinuous rather than comprising a simple correspondence (*LT*, pp. 107–9).

Eagleton also sees psychoanalysis as a form of inquiry of some value to Marxism. Eagleton refuses to regard Freud as an individualist. Rather, Freud sees the development of the individual in social and historical terms: 'What Freud produces . . . is nothing less than a materialist theory of the making of the human subject' (*LT*, p. 163). Freud's account of the dream, moreover, 'enables us to see the work of literature not as a reflection but as a form of production', working on raw materials and transforming them into a product (*LT*, p. 181). Eagleton skilfully shows how Lacan rewrites Freud on the question of the human subject, its place in society and its relationship to language.

Eagleton goes on to demonstrate how, writing under the influence of Lacan, Althusser describes the working of ideology in society. What Eagleton shows to great effect here is how the relation between Marxist and non-Marxist theory cannot be reduced to direct commensurability and is rather one of extrapolation and varying degrees of mediation.

The most controversial current 'philosophy' of the negative is deconstruction. As Michael Payne points out in the earlier section of this introduction, Eagleton distinguishes a 'right' from a 'left' deconstruction. Eagleton accepts that there are political possibilities in deconstruction. According to Eagleton, deconstruction's denial of a unity between signifier and signified, as well as its rejection of 'meaning' as self-identical and immediately present, can help us to see that certain meanings – such as those of 'freedom', 'democracy' and 'family' – are elevated by social ideologies to a privileged position as the origin or goal of other meanings. Deconstruction shows that so-called first principles are the products, rather than the foundations of, systems of meaning. Moreover, deconstruction's view of all language as metaphorical, as harbouring a surfeit over exact meaning, undermines classical structuralism's typically ideological oppositions which draw a rigid line between what is and is not acceptable, for example between truth and falsehood, sense and nonsense, reason and madness. Eagleton also points out that Derrida himself, unlike some of his acolytes, sees deconstruction as a political practice: he sees meaning, identity, intention and truth as effects of a wider history, of language, the unconscious as well as social institutions and practices.

So far, all are in accord: Hegel, Marx, non-Marxist theory and Terry Eagleton's Marxism. All view 'identity' as somehow coercive, meaning as relational, the objective world as a subjective construction and truth as institutional. One is tempted to think of the Homeric gods feasting merrily at this banquet of pure difference. But just as Marx's thought, whatever its similarities in form, has a content entirely different from Hegel's thought, so Eagleton's Marxism is marked by a specificity utterly alien to non-Marxist theory.

It is true that some of Marx's insights, such as those listed above, are superficially compatible with those of non-Marxist theory. But Marx's attacks on the various expressions of identity, such as subject, object and stable meaning, are without exception *necessarily* and internally related to the economic infrastructure. It is not just that the identification 'private property' represents the bourgeois reification of an abstract category: such reification hides the nature of private property as a product of alienated labour. It is not just that man is abstractly perceived to have no essence: man is a result of specific productive forces and specific social relations. Again, man as subject is not created in an abstractly perceived interaction with objects: he produces himself through labour. And Marx views language not as a self-enclosed or independent system but as a social practice (*GI*, pp. 18, 21, 51, 118). In each case, the 'negative' aspect of Marx's thought is necessarily, not contingently, related to his affirmative material basis.

There are at least two fundamental premises in Marx from which any Marxist criticism must begin. In the first place all forms of consciousness – religious, moral, philosophical, legal, as well as language itself – have no independent history and arise from the material activity of men. Eagleton identifies a twofold specificity of Marxist criticism: material production is regarded as the ultimate determining factor of social existence, and class struggle is viewed as the central dynamic of historical development. Eagleton adds a third, Marxist-Leninist imperative, namely a commitment to the theory and practice of political revolution (*AG*, pp. 81–2). Eagleton, as much as anyone else, is aware of the highly mediated and complex relation between base and superstructure (see *MLC*, pp. 8–10), but his aptly Marxist insistence on the primacy of material production can be seen, as we shall see, to be the basis of virtually all his attacks on non-Marxist literary theory.

The second premise is Marx's view that the class which is the ruling material force is also the ruling intellectual force: it owns the means of production both materially and mentally. In the light of this we can better understand Eagleton's statement of the tasks of a 'revolutionary literary criticism.' Such a criticism

> would dismantle the ruling concepts of 'literature', reinserting 'literary' texts into the whole field of cultural practices. It would strive to relate such 'cultural' practices to other forms of social activity, and to transform the cultural apparatuses themselves. It would articulate its 'cultural' analyses with a consistent political intervention. It would deconstruct the received hierarchies of 'literature' and transvaluate received judgments and assumptions; engage with the language and 'unconscious' of literary texts, to reveal their role in the ideological construction of the subject; and mobilize such texts . . . in a struggle to transform those subjects within a wider political context.
> (*WB*, p. 98).

But all of this subserves the 'primary task' of Marxist criticism, which is 'to actively participate in and help direct the cultural emancipation of the masses' (*WB*, p. 97). Eagleton repeatedly stresses that the starting point of theory must be a practical, political purpose and that any theory which will contribute to human emancipation through the socialist transformation of society is acceptable (*LT*, p. 211). Eagleton effectively develops Marx's premise above when he emphasizes that the 'means of production' includes the means of production of human subjectivity, which embraces a range of institutions such as 'literature'.

Eagleton regards the most difficult emancipation as that of the 'space of subjectivity', 'colonized' as it is by the dominant political order. The humanities as a whole serve an ideological function that helps to perpetuate certain forms of subjectivity. Eagleton's views here imply that for Marxist criticism, 'ideology' is a crucial focus of the link between material and mental means of production.

Eagleton affirms that the 'negation' entailed by Marxist criticism must have an affirmative material basis. There is an internal, not merely epiphenomenal, connection between practical goal and theoretical method. Hence the similarities between Marxism and 'negative' non-Marxist theories are purely superstructural: which is itself an impossible contradiction since no Marxist insight can be 'purely' superstructural. Whatever 'threat' structuralism may pose to received ideology is merely a contingent inflection of what is itself an ideological ossification of method. As Eagleton shrewdly observes, the reactionary nature of structuralism lies in the very concept of 'structure' (LT, p. 141), in the very positing of this received ideological notion as a basis of enquiry. It is only at this expense that structuralism dismantles the ruling ideologies of subjectivity. The general point here is that whatever non-Marxist theory postulates as a base or infrastructure of investigation is in fact an aspect of superstructure. Inasmuch as these theories fail to articulate their connections with the material infrastructure, they lapse into an effective, if sometimes undesired, complicity with ruling ideologies.

This is why Eagleton views non-Marxist theories as both subversive and complicit with capitalism, a contradiction inherent in their superstructural status. He arraigns, for example, structuralism's static ahistorical view of society, as well as its reduction of labour, sexuality and politics to 'language'. Structuralism, moreover, ignores both literature and language as forms of social practice and production. Its anti-humanism brackets the human subject, thereby abolishing the subject's potential as a political agent. These factors, Eagleton observes, contributed to a certain integration of structuralism into the orthodox academy (*LT*, pp. 110–15). Similarly, in Eagleton's eyes, the insights of psychoanalysis are not necessarily politically radical. For example, he asserts that the political correlative of Julia Kristeva's theories, which disrupt all fixed structures, is anarchism. And her dismantling of the unified subject is not in itself revolutionary (*LT*, pp. 189–93).

Eagleton's sustained critique of deconstruction hinges on a specifically Marxist notion of 'ideology' which he defines as a 'set . . . of values, representations and beliefs which, realised in certain material apparatuses . . . guarantee those misperceptions of the "real" which contribute to the reproduction of the dominant social relations' (*CI*, p. 54). An historical conception of the 'real' underlies any Marxist view of ideology. And we can infer from Eagleton's statement that, for Marxism, the impugnment of ideology entails an attack on identity, on all the 'identities' which comprise distorted reality and which are passed off as eternal or natural truths. These identities must be dissolved into their constitutive economic and social relations. Eagleton acknowledges the complex, internal relation between history and ideology (*CI*, pp. 80–99) but the point here is that for Marxism some notion of identity and reality (such as economic relations) must underlie this attack. For both Hegel and Marx, identity presupposes difference. But difference, in turn, presupposes identity, each being an intrinsic function of the other. But deconstruction effects a one-sided hypostatization of 'difference' alone, effectively raising it to transcendent status. Derrida states that 'the movement of différance, as that which produces different things . . . is the common root of all . . . oppositional concepts' (*POS*, p. 9). Elsewhere, Derrida defines 'différance' as 'the production of differing/deferring' (*OG*, p. 23). All of Derrida's heuristic concepts – trace, dissemination, spacing, alterity and supplement – are without exception metaphors for 'différance', which Derrida admits is based on the Hegelian notion of sublation (*POS*, p. 40), the basis of whose movement is identity-in-difference. But what does it mean to say that différance is the 'common root' of all oppositions regardless of their content? For Hegel and Marx, the content of 'difference' (which, taken historically, embraces both aspects of Derrida's differing/deferring) is not generalizable, being always historically specific. The constitutive causes (ideological, social and economic) behind various oppositions are quite different. But Derrida abstracts this historical complexity and variety into one indifferent and near-mystical cause: 'the movement of différance'. Hence Eagleton says in his essay on Adorno: 'Pure difference . . . is as blank . . . as pure identity.'

Again, there is a recognition in Derrida's work that the manifestations of identity and presence in history are coercive. But this recognition is completely abstract: he views *every* philosophical opposition, regardless of its content, as a 'violent hierarchy'. For Derrida, the base-superstructure model is one such deconstructible 'opposition'. He views the 'violence' of 'writing' as 'originary' (*OG*, p. 106). Derrida characteristically coerces historically specific texts and institutions into an abstractly uniform assailability in the name of 'writing': he defines 'grammatology' as 'the science of arbitrariness'. Small wonder that Eagleton views deconstruction as outflanking every type of knowledge 'to absolutely no effect'. Eagleton goes on:

> In the deep night of metaphysics, all cats look black. Marx is a metaphysician, and so is Schopenhauer, and so is Ronald Reagan. Has anything been gained by this manoeuvre? If it is true, is it informative? What is ideologically at stake in such homogenizing? What difference does it exist to suppress? (*WB*, p. 140)

Eagleton points out in his piece on Adorno that not all identity or unity is equally terroristic and that post-structuralism effects an 'indiscriminate conflation' of different orders of power, oppression and law. He stresses that any effective opposition to a given political order presupposes unity, solidarity and at least a sense of provisional identity. The point is that Marxist attacks on identity and ideology derive their force from their inclusion within a more comprehensive vision governed by the necessity of their relation to an economic infrastructure.

Derrida's insights, whatever their superficial opposition to prevailing orthodoxies, have merely a contingently subversive capacity since they dispense with 'identity' altogether and do not claim internal coherence except a coherence of the negative: they can affirm nothing to replace the order they 'subvert'. Eagleton points out that deconstruction's 'dispersal' of the subject, itself a politically disabling gesture, is 'purely textual': 'the infrastructure . . . for deconstruction is not de(con)structible' (*WB*, p. 139). As Derrida admits, his thought effectively arrests the Hegelian dialectic at its second phase, of 'difference': he abstracts this phase, divests it of all historical content and employs it as a transcendental principle. As Eagleton has it, deconstruction 'fails to comprehend class dialectics and turns instead to *difference*, that familiar ideological motif of the petty bourgeoisie' (*WB*, p. 134).

Hence Eagleton regards deconstruction as itself ideological. Like much post-structuralism, it effectively 'colludes with the liberal humanism it seeks to embarrass'. Eagleton insists that deconstruction reproduces common bourgeois liberal themes (the notions of 'identity' and 'substance' were, after all, attacked by Locke and Hume). Again, Eagleton shrewdly observes that many of the ideas of deconstruction are already prefigured and developed in Marxist writers such as Benjamin, Macherey and Adorno, where the empty shell of deconstructive 'difference' is imbued with political content. And because deconstruction's insights are divorced from any infrastructure, it is unaware of the historical determinants of its own *aporiai* (*WB*, p. 133).

Eagleton acknowledges the potential of deconstruction. But this cannot be read as a compromise on his part. For he is more aware than most deconstructionists that this potential is already contained, in a politically more articulate fashion, in the dialectical character of Marxism. Eagleton recognizes that there is little originality in Derrida's work. What is original to Derrida and his followers is their remorseless insistence on 'difference' as a basis of impugnment of literary and philosophical texts. Eagleton says of the 'negative': 'only a powerless petty-bourgeois intelligentsia would raise it to the solemn dignity of a philosophy' (*WB*, p. 142). The bases of Derrida's insights are already contained, on a far higher intellectual level and in the context of a far vaster historically self-conscious vision, in the writings of Hegel and Marx. Marxist criticism necessarily outstrips the Owl of Minerva; deconstruction condemns itself to lag behind.

**M. A. R. Habib**

References

The following works by Terry Eagleton are cited in the Introduction:

*Marxism and Literary Criticism* (London: New Left Books, 1976) (*MLC*).
*Criticism and Ideology* (London: New Left Books, 1976) (*CI*).
*Walter Benjamin or Towards a Revolutionary Criticism* (London: New Left Books, 1981) (*WB*).

*Literary Theory: An Introduction* (Oxford: Basil Blackwell; Minneapolis: University of Minnesota Press, 1983) (*LT*).
*The Function of Criticism* (London: New Left Books, 1984) (*FC*).
*Against the Grain: Essays 1975–1985* (London: New Left Books, 1986) (*AG*).

Other works cited

Jacques Derrida, *Of Grammatology*, trans. Gayatri Chakravorty Spivak (Baltimore and London: Johns Hopkins University Press, 1976) (*OG*).
Jacques Derrida, *Positions*, trans. Alan Bass (Chicago and London: University of Chicago Press, 1981) (*POS*).
Karl Marx, *The German Ideology*: Part One, ed. C. J. Arthur (London: Lawrence and Wishart, 1970) (*GI*).
Karl Marx, *Preface and Introduction to 'A Contribution to the Critique of Political Economy'* (Peking: Foreign Languages Press, 1976) (*CPE*).

# The Significance of Theory

I want in this lecture to theorize about theory – to engage, as they say, in 'meta-theory' – and this, at least as far as literary theory is concerned, would already seem to put me at five removes from real life. First there is the meta-theory; then the literary theory it takes as its object of enquiry; then literary criticism, which much literary theory reflects on; then literature, the object of critical investigation; and then 'real life', the object of literature itself. It is difficult to engage in this enterprise, in other words, without feeling that one is falling off the edge. But of course this sharp polarity between 'theory' and 'life' is surely misleading. All social life is in some sense theoretical: even such apparently concrete, unimpeachable statements as 'pass the salt' or 'I've just put the cat out' engage theoretical propositions of a kind, controvertible statements about the nature of the world. This is, admittedly, theory of a pretty low level, hardly of an Einsteinian grandeur; but propositions such as 'this is a beer mug' depend on the assumption that the object in question will smash if dropped from a certain height rather than put out a small daintily coloured parachute, and if it did the latter rather than the former then we would have to revise the proposition. And just as all social life is theoretical, so all theory is a real social practice.

What distinguishes the human animal from its fellow creatures is that it moves within a world of meaning – or, more simply, that it inhabits a *world*, rather than just a physical space. Human life is sign-making – 'significant' – existence. It is not that, unlike other animals, we have physical activities but signs as well; it is that living among signs transforms the whole meaning of the phrase 'physical activity'. The activity of a human animal is not behaviour plus something else; because we have that something else – language – our biological behaviour is transfigured into history. I do not mean to suggest that we do not share a great deal of importance with other animals, or that language is the only way history comes about; we could not have history, for example, if we could not labour in certain ways, ways which language helps to make possible. But the edge we have over other creatures makes a vital difference to the activities we share with them. For one thing, it makes our whole existence a good deal more precarious. Because we deploy signs, we can overreach our bodies to the point where we can undo them, as in warfare. If squirrels, as far as we know, are not at this moment busy secretly constructing nuclear weapons, it is not particularly because they are a nicer crowd than we are but because they cannot deploy our kind of signs. Their monotonous, species-determined biological existence is a good deal safer and more stable than ours. One reason why we have theories is in order to stabilize our signs. In this sense all theories, even revolutionary ones, have something conservative about them. But if we extinguished this precariousness which language brings us we would extirpate our creativity too, and so, as they say in Britain, you have to take the kicks with the ha'pence.

If all human existence is in some sense theoretical, then theory is an activity which goes on all the time, even when putting the cat out and smashing beer mugs. But when you get a really virulent outbreak of theory, on an epidemic scale, as we have been witnessing in the literary institutions for the past twenty years or so, then you can be sure that something is amiss. Since this sounds the kind of statement more likely to be advanced by Professor Bloom than by myself, I should perhaps explain it. (I mean the Professor Bloom of the University of Chicago, not the real Professor Bloom.) For much of the time, our intellectual and other activities bowl along fairly serenely, and in this situation no great expenditure of theoretical energy is usually necessary. But there may come a point where these taken-for-granted activities begin to falter, log-jam, come unstuck, run into trouble, and it is at these points that theory proves necessary. Theory on a dramatic scale happens when it is both possible and necessary for it to do so – when the traditional rationales which have silently underpinned our daily practices stand in danger of being discredited, and need either to be revised or discarded. This may come about for reasons internal to those practices, or because of certain external pressures, or more typically because of a combination of both. Theory is just a practice forced into a new form of self-reflectiveness on account of certain grievous problems it has encountered. Like small lumps on the neck, it is a symptom that all is not well.

Whether and when this actually happens to a human practice is a highly variable matter. A long time ago, for example, people used simply to drop things from time to time. But nowadays we have physicists to inform us of the laws of gravity by which objects fall; philosophers to doubt whether there are really any discrete objects to be dropped at all; sociologists to explain how all this dropping is really the consequence of urban pressures; psychologists to suggest that we are really trying to drop our parents; poets to write about how all this dropping is symbolic of death; and critics to argue that it is a sign of the poet's castration anxiety. Now dropping can never be the same again. We can never return to the happy garden where we simply wandered around dropping things all day without a care in the world. What has happened, rather, is that the practice has now been forced to take itself as its own object of enquiry. Theory is just human activity bending back upon itself, constrained into a new kind of self-reflexivity. And in absorbing this self-reflexivity, the activity itself will be transformed, as the production of literature is altered by the existence of literary criticism.

This, however, would seem to involve a curious paradox. For one of the effects of rendering our practices self-conscious in this way, of formalizing the tacit understandings by which they operate, may well be to disable them. Perhaps we only did what we did because we **were** *not* conscious of the problematical assumptions underlying our conduct. Indeed many theorists, from Friedrich Nietzsche to Sigmund Freud and Louis Althusser, have claimed that such amnesia or oblivion is an essential condition for any purposive action whatsoever. To objectify a procedure is to turn it into a potential object of contestation, which is why it is always safer for a ruling order to follow the English path and not do anything as vulgar and perilous as actually committing its constitution to paper. If you think too hard about how to kiss someone you are bound to make a mess of it. Theory, then, potentially destabilizes social life; but I have said already that it is also a conservative force. It is conservative in so far as it often seeks to supply us with new rationales for what we do, ordering and formalizing our meanings; but it cannot do this without making us freshly conscious of what we do, and this may always raise the possibility that we should do something else for a change.

The object of theory is, in a vastly broad sense, 'history'; but this formulation will not quite do, since theorizing is itself of course an historical event. An act of theory takes history as its target, but then finds itself joining the very history it ponders, altering it in the process. In order to understand *this* occurrence, we would need another act of theorizing by which to do so; but this 'meta-theorizing' is in turn an historical event, will be absorbed into the history upon which it reflects, and will thus require yet another act of theory to show how all *this* comes about. We find ourselves, in other words, in an infinite regress, as 'theory' and 'history' chase each other's tails in an apparently ceaseless dialectic. The only way we could arrest this chain would be by arriving at the Theory of Theories, the Grand Global Theory which would not itself constitute an historical event. This solution has only one drawback, namely that it is impossible.

The reason why we are still afflicted by the fall-out of the great theoretical explosion which has taken place over the past two decades is that we have still not solved the problem of which this outburst of theory is the symptom. That problem has in my view nothing to do in the first place with literature or literary criticism; it has to do with the role of the 'humanities' in late capitalist societies. Theory would not have had the pervasive, perturbing effect it has had if it were simply a matter of whether to talk about signifiers rather than symbols or semantic overdetermination rather than poetic texture. Nobody outside a few thousand politically unimportant people is much concerned with these matters, and the fact that a few years ago in Britain a controversy about structuralism at Cambridge University made it onto the front page of the 'quality' newspapers has more to say about the brittle glamour of Cambridge than the hunger of the masses for a correct solution to the structuralist problem. (A *Punch* cartoon at the time portrayed a working man reading his morning newspaper and being asked by his wife: 'Have they caught the Cambridge structuralist yet?', evidently under the impression that he was a murderer on the loose.) If theory matters, it is surely because it touches a sore point at the very centre of Western society: the fact that the humanities are in one sense exceedingly important to its corporate existence, and in another sense hardly matter at all. It is hardly surprising that the guardians of the humanities – literary critics and others – should experience under these circumstances what Jacques Lacan might have called a 'fading of the subject' or crisis of identity, and seek anxiously for solutions to it through new modes of self-reflection.

The phrase 'the crisis of the humanities' is a good instance of what the rhetoricians call tautology. For crisis is as native to the humanities as haggis is to Scotland, and has dogged them from the very outset. It is not that there is an assured body of values known as the humanities which rather recently hit some worrying problems; on the contrary, crisis and the humanities were born at a stroke. Indeed the very idea of constructing a certain privileged enclave called the humanities, relatively marooned from the common activities of social life, in which the most precious values of that life might be nurtured and contemplated, is part of the problem rather than of the solution. Historically speaking, the idea of the humanities, at least in the modern period, arises at a point where certain kinds of positive human values are felt to be increasingly under threat from a philistine, crassly materialist society, and so must be marked off from that degraded social arena in a double gesture of elevation and isolation. How *could* the humanities not be in crisis in social orders where it is perfectly clear, whatever their own protestations to the contrary, that the only supremely valuable activity is one of turning a fast buck? Yet it is just as clear that the humanities are not thereby a mere hypocrisy, icing on the cake of capitalism; on the contrary, they still have an enormously significant role to play in the construction and reproduction of forms of subjectivity which that society finds ideologically indispensable. Most human societies, perhaps all of them, carve out some sacred discursive space within the clamour of their more instrumental idioms, where what can be reflected upon for a precious moment is not this or that particular technique or utilitarian practice but the very meaning of the human as such. You may call this space myth or religion or a certain kind of philosophizing or increasingly, in our own epoch, literature. How blessed to be able to savour the human *as such*, shorn of its specific social, sexual, racial and historical embodiments! And what a pity that this whole notion is no more than an ideological myth in its turn.

That this brand of transcendental humanism is indeed no more than a myth was becoming painfully evident throughout the 1960s – the period in which literary theory as we have it today first took off the ground. (Many of the actual theories in question, of course, run back far beyond that date; but it was in that era that they were refurbished and reconstituted into the loosely connected set of discourses which we now know as literary theory.) At the height of capitalist consumerism, American imperialism and the Civil Rights movement, it was becoming more and more difficult to conceal the fact that those areas of disinterested humane enquiry known as academic institutions were in fact locked directly into the structures of technological dominance, military violence and ideological legitimation. A new, more socially heterogeneous student body, who could not be expected any longer spontaneously to share the cultural class-assumptions of their teachers, thus effected a kind of practical 'estrangement' of those assumptions, which forced them in turn into the new forms of critical self-reflection I have talked about already. 'Theory' was born as a political intervention, whatever academic respectability it may since have achieved.

No theory, however, has built into it a self-evident political orientation, any more than has a literary form. This is not to say that theories and literary forms are politically *neutral* – rather that they are politically *polyvalent*, capable of generating a multiplicity of sometimes quite contradictory social effects. It was shrewd of Goebbels, Hitler's Minister of Propaganda, to offer a job under the Nazis to Erwin Piscator, Germany's greatest Marxist theatre director and mentor of Bertolt Brecht. Goebbels saw quite correctly that there was no reason why the theatrical technology which Piscator had harnessed to the cause of an emancipatory politics should not be hijacked for quite opposite political ends. Theory suffers from a similar ambivalence. If the humanities are in deep trouble, then theory may either be used to expose their disreputable ideological roots, or deployed to refurbish them in glamorous new ways. Theory can be seen as providing a flagging literary critical industry with a much-needed boost of spiritual plant and capital, largely imported from the nations of the European Economic Community. In the postwar years, cultural modernism had become increasingly institutionalized in the West, as *Ulysses* entered the university syllabuses and Schoenberg sidled regularly into the concert halls. Theory was then one place in which that subversive modernist impulse could take refuge: what was developing was not simply a 'theory of modernism' but, more excitingly, a 'modernist theory'. But that in its turn proved progressively vulnerable to incorporation, as Bakhtin and Benjamin assumed their revered places beside Balzac and Beckett in the academic bookshops.

Speaking as an outsider, it seems to me that the most quintessentially American utterance these days, apart from 'Have a nice day', is 'They can incorporate anything!' American liberals and radicals tend understandably to be something of a gloomy, fatalistic bunch, painfully conscious as they are of the rapidity with which even the most revolutionary work of art can be placed in the lobby of the Chemical Bank, or of the alacrity with which the Pentagon can hire its clutch of semioticians and deconstructionists. This was not, on the whole, a problem which greatly dogged the revolutionary avant-gardes of the early Soviet Union or the Weimar Republic. How idealist to imagine that art, or theory, could in itself resist political power! If your cherished revolutionary artefacts could be integrated into the system, then this surely only meant one thing: not that they were not outrageous or subversive enough, but either that they had no real roots in a mass oppositional political movement, or that they did, but (as with the Soviet and Weimar cases) those movements were finally defeated. The question of 'incorporation' is a question of politics, not in the first place of theory or culture. If the current system continues, then it is no doubt true that there is in principle no theory or cultural production which it cannot turn to its own squalid ends. If an oppositional movement succeeds, then the ruling order will be unable to incorporate a thing because it will have been incorporated by its opponents. The one thing which that order cannot incorporate is its own defeat. Let it try putting *that* in the lobby of its banks.

The question of the uses of theory, then, is in the first place a political rather than intellectual one. Literary critics do not in my view divide most importantly between those who are enthusiastic about theory and those who regard it as the final death rattle of the Free World. They divide, rather, between those who understand what Walter Benjamin meant when he declared that there was no document of civilization which was not also a record of barbarism, and those who do not. You do not need 'theory' to understand the meaning of this claim; many of those subjected to barbarism, bereft of academic education, understand its meaning perfectly well. You may, however, require theory to work out some of its implications. Benjamin did not presumably mean by his statement that documents of civilization were nothing *but* records of barbarism. He meant that there is a way of reading – difficult and delicate – which can, so to speak,

X-ray the text in order to allow to emerge through its affirmative pronouncements the shadowy lineaments of the toil, misery and wretchedness which made it possible in the first place. The only good reason for being a socialist, in my opinion, is that one cannot quite overcome one's amazement that the fate of the vast majority of men and women who have ever lived and died has been, and still is today, one of fruitless, unremitting labour. As Bertolt Brecht might have said, it is the non-necessity of this which is its tragedy. 'Culture' has its dubious roots in this unprepossessing soil, and like human beings themselves is always eager to repress its own disreputable origins, fantasize that it sprang fully fledged from its own loins. A materialist criticism is one which seeks to undo this Oedipal fantasy and remind culture of its criminal parentage. What method, theory, approach or technique it employs for these ends is an entirely secondary matter.

Once an emancipatory theory has succeeded in this task, then there will be nothing left for it to do and it should allow itself to wither away as quickly and decently as possible. It is a mistake, in other words, to imagine that emancipatory theorists – socialists, feminists and others – hold their beliefs somewhat in the way that Buddhists and vegetarians do. The latter presumably wish to remain faithful to their beliefs for as long as they survive; the former wish to get rid of them as soon as possible. Their aim is to help bring about the material conditions in which their theories would no longer be essential, or even, after a while, fully intelligible. If there are political radicals around in fifty years time it will be a grim prospect. All emancipatory theory thus has built into it a kind of self-destruct device, and moves under the sign of irony. In the just society, there would be no need for radical theorists to engage in laborious expositions of the social mechanisms by which one group of individuals comes systematically to dominate another, since people would just be horrified or incredulous at the very thought that this could happen. Those who regard such a view as impossibly romantic or utopian forget that there are millions of people in the world today who have no understanding of systems of domination, and who might well find the whole idea appalling. These people are known as children. Children make the best theorists, since they have not yet been educated into accepting our routine social practices as 'natural,' and so insist on posing to those practices the most embarrassingly general and fundamental questions, regarding them with a wondering estrangement which we adults have long forgotten. Since they do not yet grasp our social practices as inevitable, they do not see why we might not do things entirely differently. 'Where does capitalism come from, mummy?' is thus the prototypical theoretical question, one which usually receives what one might term a Wittgensteinian reply: 'This is just the way we do things, dear.' It is those children who remain discontent with this shabby parental response who tend to grow up to be emancipatory theorists, unable to conquer their amazement at what everyone else seems to take for granted. Bertolt Brecht used to instruct his actors to perform with such an amazement well in mind, in what is known as the 'alienation effect'. Good social actors are those who have come spontaneously to internalize their allotted roles, and thus tend to be awarded medals for good citizenship. Brecht, for his part, much preferred amateur actors, since they were generally less skilled at such spontaneous internalization and so continually created unwitting alienation effects. The point of emancipatory theory is to regress us to childhood, or encourage us to be inept actors. Theory is often felt to be difficult because it uses phrases like 'hermeneutical phenomenology', and it is certainly the case that no discourse devoted to exposing the complex mechanisms by which a society works can hope to sound like the kind of thing one might hear on the top of a bus. 'Jargon' just means a language not natural to *me*; but one person's jargon is another person's ordinary language. The true difficulty of theory, however, springs not from this sophistication, but from exactly the opposite – from its demand that we return to childhood by rejecting what seems natural and refusing to be fobbed off with shifty answers from well-meaning elders.

Imagine a group of people trapped, Buñuel-like, in a room, discussing possible ways of getting out. A new person enters – this room, let us conveniently imagine, has only a one-way obstacle – and settles down to listen to the talk. After a while it occurs to her that though some of the talk is indeed constructive, much of it is more of a symptom of the situation than a strategic response to it. Perhaps these people are actually fearful of leaving the room, and their wranglings are to this extent a form of displacement. The newly arrived member of the group is then faced with a problem. What she needs to do is fashion a form of discursive intervention which will somehow succeed in illuminating the relation between the talk and the situation; she must find some 'meta-discourse' (which may only be such for these particular purposes) which will persuade her trapped fellows to grasp their talk as bound up with their material conditions rather than simply as a potential solution to them. But any statement she makes is clearly in danger of merely being absorbed into the already-established circuit of discussion, heard as just another helpful suggestion rather than as an attempt to transform the entire scenario. This newly arrived individual, note, does not need to be 'disinterested', and indeed cannot possibly be so: why then would she be anxious to intervene? It is not necessarily that she is in possession of some superior knowledge; it is just that she is following a different rule from the others, a rule which includes the injunction: 'always listen to discourse as at least in part symptomatic of the material conditions within which it goes on, rather than as a thing in itself.' In this situation, the new individual is the theorist, and the ones already in the room are the ideologues. Those radicals or liberals who feel somewhat uncomfortable about such an example because it seems to suggest that the theorist is 'superior' to the rest should remember that the corollary of rejecting a title ever to tell anyone else anything helpful is rejecting ever being told.

Despite this claim to superiority, emancipatory theorists are on the whole unlikely to fall prey to megalomania. They are unlikely to do so because their own materialist theories inform them that, in any process of actual emancipation, their own role is hardly a central one. This is not to say that those in need of emancipation do not crucially require self-reflection – that since the theorist's role is hardly central, he or she has no role at all. It is simply to insist that political emancipation, like eating or drinking, is by definition (not just contingently) an activity one can only carry out for oneself. And this is partly because the most difficult form of emancipation is always a matter of freeing ourselves from ourselves. Liberal humanism is fond of imagining an inner space within the human subject where he or she is most significantly free. A sophisticated liberal humanist will not of course deny that human subjects are externally or even internally afflicted by all kinds of grievous determinants and constraints; it is just that what these forces seek to determine and constrain is some transcendental core of inner freedom. The bad news for the liberal humanist is that this 'inner space' is actually where we are least free. If we were simply hedged round with oppressive powers, we would no doubt have a reasonable chance of putting up some active resistance to them. But no dominant political order is likely to survive very long if it does not intensively colonize the space of subjectivity itself. No oppressive power which does not succeed in entwining itself with people's real needs and desires, engaging with vital motifs of their actual experience, is likely to be very effective. Power succeeds by persuading us to desire and collude with it; and this process is not merely an enormous confidence trick, since we really do have needs and desires which such power, however partially and distortedly, is able to fulfil. Among the various modes of production of any social order is the mode of production of human subjects, or forms of subjectivity; and this mode of production is made up of a whole range of institutions, from church and family to school and culture. The apparatuses of production of forms of subjectivity are just as historically variable as modes of producing economic goods. Literature, in our day, is one such (somewhat subsidiary) apparatus, devoted to the inculcation of certain affective codes and disciplines within subjects. It is in this way that it has a part to play in the more general processes of political power.

To claim that the 'inner space' is an inappropriate metaphor for picturing human freedom is not, of course, to deny that freedom's existence. It is just to deny that human freedom can ever be usefully thought of as 'inner'. Rather, it is the capacity to make something of that which makes us, and the portmanteau word for that is history. For power to inscribe itself effectively within subjectivity there must be something in it for individuals themselves. We must be in some ways gratified as well as frustrated by it; otherwise the state will be forced to have recourse to naked coercion, thus suffering a drastic loss of ideological credibility. But if there is not enough gratification for individuals, then they will demonstrate their freedom dramatically by rebellion. It is quite as certain that people will rebel in the long run against forms of oppressive power which allow them too few fulfilments, as that they will tend to submit to such power when those fulfilments are available. Individuals are in this sense as naturally revolutionary as they are naturally conservative. But the run can, of course, be a long one; and meanwhile, in societies like Britain and the USA whose rulers desire not simply to combat radical ideas but to erase them from living memory, 'theory' is necessary, among other reasons, for keeping those energies warm.

# Art after Auschwitz: *Adorno's Political Aesthetics*

An 'aesthetic' thought is one true to the opacity of its object. But if thought is conceptual, and so general, how can 'aesthetic thought' be other than an oxymoron? How can the mind not betray the object in the very act of possessing it, struggling to register its density and recalcitrance at just the point it impoverishes it to some pallid universal? It would seem that the crude linguistic instruments with which we lift a thing towards us, preserving as much as possible of its unique quality, simply succeed in pushing it further away. In order to do justice to the qualitative moments of the thing, thought must thicken its own texture, grow gnarled and close-grained; but in doing so it becomes a kind of object in its own right, sheering off from the phenomenon it hoped to encircle. As Theodor Adorno remarks: 'the consistency of its performance, the density of its texture, helps the thought to miss the mark'.[1]

Dialectical thinking seeks to grasp whatever is heterogeneous to thought as a moment of thought itself, 'reproduced in thought itself as its immanent contradiction'.[2] But since one risks eradicating that heterogeneity in the very act of reflecting upon it, this enterprise is always teetering on the brink of blowing itself up. Adorno has a kind of running solution to this dilemma, and that is style. What negotiates this contradiction is the crabbed, rebarbative practice of writing itself, a discourse pitched into a constant state of crisis, twisting and looping back on itself, struggling in the structure of every sentence to avoid at once a 'bad' immediacy of the object and the false self-identity of the concept. Dialectical thought digs the object loose from its illusory self-identity, but thereby risks liquidating it within some ghastly concentration camp of the Absolute Idea; and Adorno's provisional response to this problem is a set of guerrilla raids on the inarticulable, a style of philosophizing which frames the object conceptually but manages by some cerebral acrobatics to glance sideways at what gives such generalized identity the slip. Every sentence of his texts is thus forced to work overtime; each phrase must become a little masterpiece or miracle of dialectics, fixing a thought in the second before it disappears into its own contradictions. Like Benjamin's, this style is a constellatory one, each sentence a kind of crystallized conundrum from which the next is strictly non-deducible, a tight-meshed economy of epigrammatic *aperçus* in which every part is somehow autonomous yet intricately related to its fellows. All Marxist philosophers are supposed to be dialectical thinkers; but with Adorno one can feel the sweat and strain of this mode alive in every phrase, in a language rammed up against silence where the reader has no sooner registered the one-sidedness of some proposition than the opposite is immediately proposed.

The complaint that we live in some disabling gap between concept and thing is in one sense a productive insight, in another sense a kind of category error. Why should thoughts be like things, any more than the notion of freedom should resemble a ferret? Behind this nominalist plaint that words violate the quiddity of things lies a nostalgia for the happy garden in which every object wore its own word in much the way that every flower flaunts its peculiar scent. But the fact that language universalizes is part of what it is, not some lapse or limit from which we might hope to be cured. It is not a defect of the word 'foot' that it refers to more feet than my own two, careless of the peculiarity of my own personal pair. To mourn the non-particularism of language is as misplaced as regretting that one cannot tune into the World Cup on a washing machine. The concept of a thing is not some pale mental replica of it, damagingly bereft of the thing's sensuous life, but a set of social practices – a way of doing something with the word which denotes the thing. A concept is no more like an object than the use of a spanner is like a spanner. Poetry strives to phenomenalize language, but this, as Adorno sees, is entirely self-defeating, since the more it labours to be like the thing, the more it becomes a thing in its own right, which resembles the object no more than a squirrel resembles the slave trade. Perhaps it is a pity that we lack a word to capture the unique aroma of coffee – that our speech is wizened and anaemic, remote from the taste and feel of reality. But how could a word, as opposed to a pair of nostrils, capture the aroma of anything, and is it a matter of failure that it does not?

This is not to suggest, on the other hand, that Adorno is mistaken in believing our concepts to be reified and inadequate, adrift from our sensuous practice; indeed it is precisely in his concern to return thought to the body, lend it something of the body's feel and fullness, that he is, in the most traditional sense of the word, an aesthetician. His work, however, heralds one momentous shift of emphasis in that tradition. For what the body signals to Adorno is not first of all pleasure but suffering. In the shadow of Auschwitz it is in sheer physical wretchedness, in human shapes at the end of their tether, that the body once more obstrudes itself into the rarefied world of the philosophers. 'If thought is not measured by the extremity that eludes the concept', he remarks in *Negative Dialectics*, 'it is from the outset in the nature of the musical accompaniment with which the SS liked to drown out the screams of its victims.'[3] Even this intolerable agony, of course, must somehow engage the idea of pleasurable well-being, for how could we measure suffering without such an implicit norm? But if there is any basis at all for a universal history, it is not a tale of cumulative happiness but, as Adorno comments, the narrative that leads from the slingshot to the megaton bomb. 'The One and All that keeps rolling on to this day – with occasional breathing spells – would teleologically be the absolute of suffering.'[4] There is indeed, as Marx recognized, a singular global story which weaves all men and women into its fabric, from the Stone Age to Star Wars; but it is a tale of scarcity and oppression, not of success – a fable, as Adorno puts it, of permanent catastrophe. The body has lived on, despite the depredations of instrumental reason; but in the fascist death-camps those depredations have now accomplished their deadliest work. For Adorno, there can be no real history after such an event, just the twilight or aftermath in which time still moves listlessly, vacuously on, even though humanity itself has come to a full stop. For a Jew like Adorno, there can only be the guilty mystery that one is still, by some oversight, alive. Adorno's politics of the body is thus the very reverse of Bakhtinian: the only image of the body which is more than a blasphemous lie is stark and skeletal, the poor forked creature of Beckettian humanity. In the wake of the Nazis, the whole aesthetic concern with sensation, with the innocent creaturely life, has become irreversibly disfigured – for fascism, as Adorno argues in *Minima Moralia*, 'was the absolute sensation . . . in the Third Reich the abstract horror of news and rumour was enjoyed as the only stimulus sufficient to incite a momentary glow in the weakened sensorium of the masses.'[5] Sensation in such conditions becomes a matter of commodified shock-value regardless of content: everything can now become pleasure,

just as the desensitized morphine addict will grab indiscriminately at any drug. To posit the body and its pleasures
as an unquestionably affirmative category is a dangerous
illusion in a social order which reifies and regulates
corporeal pleasure for its own ends just as relentlessly as
it colonizes the mind. Any return to the body which fails
to reckon this truth into its calculations will be merely
naïve; and it is to Adorno's credit that, conscious of this
as he is, he does no flinch from trying to redeem what he
calls the 'somatic moment' of cognition, that irreducible
dimension which accompanies all our acts of consciousness
but can never be exhausted by them. The aesthetic project
must not be abandoned, even if its terms of reference have
been permanently tainted by fascism and 'mass' society.

The inadequation between thing and concept is importantly two-way. If the concept can never appropriate the
object without leaving a remainder, then it is also true
that the object – 'freedom', for example – fails to achieve
the fullness promised by its concept. What prevents us
from fully possessing the world is also what invests that
world with some wan hope, the lack which spurs the thing
out of its self-identity so as to rise to what it might in
principle become. An identity of concept and phenomenon
is for Adorno 'the primal form of ideology',[6] and Auschwitz
confirmed the philosopheme of pure identity as death; but
for him there is always another side to the story, unlike
those present-day theorists whose pluralism would seem to
wear a little thin when it comes to recognizing that identity,
too, can have its value. 'Living in the rebuke that the
thing is not identical with the concept', Adorno writes, 'is
the concept's longing to become identical with the thing.
This is how the sense of non-identity contains identity.
The supposition of identity is indeed the ideological
element of pure thought all the way through to formal
logic; but hidden in it is also the truth moment of ideology,
the pledge that there should be no contradiction, no

antagonism.'[7] It would be a grim prospect if the concept of liberty or equality really was identical with the poor travesty of it we observe around us. Our current conceptions of identity can be shaken not only by difference, but by an identity which would be otherwise – which belongs to the political future, but which reverberates as a faint echo or pledge of reconciliation even in our most paranoid present-day identifications. That such a thought is scandalous to the mere celebration of difference is a measure of its subversive force.

Classical dialectical thought, for which 'contradiction is non-identity under the sign of identity',[8] is perfectly capable of registering the heterogeneous: it simply measures it by its own principles of unity, thereby coolly reckoning in to itself what it has just acknowledged to be irreducibly exterior. What it extracts from the object is only what was already in any case, a thought. Adorno, on the other hand, believes with the deconstructive theory he prefigures almost in its entirety in 'identity's dependence on the non-identical.'[9] The indissoluble must be brought into its own in concepts, not subsumed under an abstract idea in that generalized barter of the mind which mirrors the equalizing exchanges of the market place. For Adorno as for Nietzsche, identificatory thought has its source in the eyes and stomach, the limbs and mouth. The prehistory of such violent appropriation of otherness is that of the early human predator out to devour the not-I. Dominative reason is 'the belly turned mind',[10] and such atavistic rage against otherness is the hallmark of every high-minded idealism. All philosophy, even that which intends freedom, bears within itself like a primordial urge the coercion by which society prolongs its oppressive existence. But for Adorno there is always another story, and this particular argument is no exception. The coerciveness of the identity principle, installed at the heart of Enlightenment reason, is also what prevents thought from lapsing into mere license; and in its own pathological way it parodies, as well as forestalls, some authentic reconciliation of subject and object. What is required, then, is 'a rational critique of reason, not its banishment or abolition'[11] – hardly a surprising position for one whom the abolition of reason drove into exile. The problem is how to prise loose the grip of an insane rationality without allowing the slightest opening to some barbarous irrationalism.

This project involves thinking through the relations between universal and particular once again, this time on some model other than that of the singular law which flattens all specificity to its own image and likeness. If Adorno's style is tortuous and unsettling, it is partly because these relations are themselves fraught and unquiet, forever likely to slip out of focus as he steers a precarious course between the Scylla of blind particularism and the Charybdis of the tyrannical concept. 'Unreflective nominalism', he writes, 'is as wrong as the realism that equips a fallible language with the attributes of a revealed one.'[12] The way to avoid an oppressive totality is through the constellation:

> we are not to philosophise about concrete things; we are to philosophise, rather out of those things . . . there is no step-by-step progression from the concepts to a more general cover concept. Instead, the concepts enter into a constellation. . . . By gathering around the object of cognition, the concepts potentially determine the object's interior. They attain, in thinking, what was necessarily excised from thinking.[13]

Paradoxically, however, the circumvention of totality is only possible because of it. If it is true that 'objectively – not just through the knowing subject – the whole which theory expresses is contained in the individual object to be analysed',[14] this is because in an increasingly administered, manipulated world 'the more tightly the network of general definitions covers its objects, the greater will be the tendency of individual facts to be direct transparencies of their universals, and the greater the yield a viewer obtains precisely by micrological immersion'.[15] We may forget about totality, but totality, for good or ill, will not forget about us, even in our most microscopic meditations. If we can unpack the whole from the most humble particular, glimpse eternity in a grain of sand, this is because we inhabit a social order which tolerates particularity only as an obedient instantiation of the universal. We must no longer aim thought directly at this totality, but neither should we surrender ourselves to some pure play of difference, which would be quite as monotonous as the dreariest self-identity and indeed finally indistinguishable from it.[16] We must rather grasp the truth that the individual is both more and less than its general definition, and that the principle of identity is always self-contradictory, perpetuating non-identity in damaged, suppressed form as a condition of its being.

The place where particular and universal consort most harmoniously is traditionally supposed to be art. The aesthetic is that privileged condition in which the law of the whole is nothing but the interrelations of the parts. But if this is true, then each part is still governed by what is in effect a total system; and it is this chiasmus of the aesthetic which Adorno will try to outflank. In art, the emancipation of the particular would seem merely to lead to a new form of global subordination; and it is surely not difficult to see how this contradiction corresponds to the amphibious nature of bourgeois society, in which the ideal of an interchange of autonomous individuals is constantly thwarted by the persistence of political domination. The work of art appears free from the viewpoint of its particular elements, but unfree from the standpoint of the law which surreptitiously marshals them into unity. In a similar way, the individual subject is free from the viewpoint of the market place, but not from the perspective of the state which violently or manipulatively preserves that market place in being. Adorno seeks to recast the relations between global and specific by finding in the aesthetic an impulse to reconciliation between them which must never quite come off, a utopian yearning for identity which must deny itself under pain of fetishism and idolatry. The work of art suspends identity without cancelling it, broaches and breaches it simultaneously, refusing at once to underwrite antagonism or supply false consolation. If its movement is thus one of perpetual deferral, this is less because of some ontological condition of language than because of the Judaeo-Marxist prohibition on the fashioning of graven images of a political future which must none the less be remembered.

Art may thus offer an alternative to thought, which for the Adorno of *Dialectic of Enlightenment* is inherently pathological. In characteristically monistic style, he refuses to distinguish between different forms of rationality: all rationality is instrumental, and simply to think is therefore to violate and victimize. A valid theory could only be one which thinks against itself, undoes its every act, achieves a frail evocation of that which its own discursivity denies. Emancipatory thought is an enormous irony, an indispensable absurdity in which the concept is at once deployed and disowned, no sooner posited than sur-mounted, illuminating truth only in the dim glare of light by which it self-destructs. The utopia of knowledge would be to open up the non-conceptual to concepts without rendering it equivalent to them; and this involves reason somehow hauling itself up by its own bootstraps, for if thought is intrinsically violatory how has the thought which thinks this truth not already fallen victim to the very crime it denounces?

If emancipatory thought is a scandalous contradiction,

so in a different sense is the dominative reason it seems to unlock. Historically speaking, such reason helps to release the self from its enslavement to myth and Nature; but in a devastating irony the drive to this enabling autonomy itself hardens into a kind of ferocious animal compulsion, subverting the very freedom it sets in place. In repressing its own inner nature in the name of independence, the subject finds itself throttling the very spontaneity which its break with Nature supposedly set free – so that the upshot of all this strenuous labour of individuation is an undermining of the ego from within, as the self gradually implodes into some empty, mechanical conformity. The forging of the ego is thus an ambivalently emancipatory and repressive event; and the unconscious is marked by a similar duality, promising us some blissful sensuous fulfilment but threatening at every moment to thrust us back to that archaic, undifferentiated state in which we are no longer subjects at all, let alone liberated ones. Fascism then gives us the worst of all possible worlds: the torn, wounded Nature over which an imperious reason has trampled returns with a vengeance as blood, guts and soil, but in the cruellest of ironies is now harnessed to that brutally instrumental reason itself, in an unholy coupling of the atavistic and futuristic, savage irrationalism and technological dominion. For Adorno, the self is rent by an internal fissure, and the name for the experience of it is suffering. How, then, is the identity of the subject, which is a constitutive moment of its freedom and autonomy, to be combined with the sensuousness and spontaneity on which the drive to autonomy has inflicted such grievous damage?

Adorno's solution to this riddle is the aesthetic – in so far, that is, as art is now possible at all. Modernism is art forced into mute self-contradiction; and the source of this internal impasse lies in art's contradictory material status within bourgeois society. Culture is deeply locked into the structure of commodity production; but one effect of this is to release it into a certain ideological autonomy, hence allowing it to speak against the very social order with which it is guiltily complicit. It is this complicity which spurs art into protest, but which also strikes that protest agonized and ineffectual, formal gesture rather than irate polemic. Art can only hope to be valid if it provides an implicit critique of the conditions which produce it – a validation which, in evoking art's privileged remoteness from such conditions, instantly invalidates itself. Conversely, art can only be authentic if it silently acknowledges how deeply it is compromised by what it opposes; but to press this logic too far is precisely to undermine its authenticity. The aporia of modernist culture lies in its plaintive, stricken attempt to turn autonomy (the free-standing nature of the aesthetic work) against autonomy (its functionless status as commodity on the market); what warps it into non-self-identity is the inscription of its own material conditions on its interior. It would seem that art must now either abolish itself entirely – the audacious strategy of the avant-garde – or hover indecisively between life and death, subsuming its own impossibility into itself.

At the same time, it is this internal slippage or hiatus within the art work, this impossibility of ever coinciding exactly with itself, which provides the very source of its critical power, in a world where objects lie petrified in their monotonously self-same being, doomed to the hell of being no more than themselves. It is as though Adorno, who was never much entranced by the avant-garde and can hardly bring himself to say a polite word about Bertolt Brecht, seizes upon the dilemma of culture in late capitalism and presses it to a calculated extreme, so that in a defiant reversal it is the very impotence of an autonomous art which will be wrenched into its finest aspect, victory snatched from the jaws of defeat as art's shaming privilege and futility is carried to a Beckettian limit and at that point begins to veer on its axis to become (negative) critique. Like Beckett, Adorno maintains a compact with failure, which is where for both Jew and Irishman all authenticity must start. An artistic vacuity which is the product of social conditions, and so part of the problem, can come by some strange logic to figure as a creative solution. The more art suffers this relentless *kenosis*, the more powerfully it speaks to its historical epoch; the more it turns its back on social issues, the more politically eloquent it grows. There is something perversely self-defeating abut this aesthetic, which takes its cue from a notable contradiction of 'autonomous' culture – the fact that art's independence of social life permits it a critical force which that same autonomy tends to cancel out. 'Neutralisation', as Adorno comments, 'is the social price art pays for its autonomy.'[17] The more socially dissociated art becomes, the more scandalously subversive and utterly pointless it is. For art to *refer*, even protestingly, is for it to become instantly collusive with what it opposes; negation negates itself because it cannot help positing the very object it desires to destroy. Any positive enunciation is compromised by the very fact of being such; and it follows that what one is left with is the purest imprint of the gesture of negation itself, which must never stray from the elevated level of form to anything as lowly as content. So it is that Adorno comes to rehearse with a new inflection all the reactionary clichés which a committed art customarily attracts, railing at its supposed schematism and reductivism. The most profoundly political work is one that is entirely silent about politics, as for some the greatest poet is one who has never sullied his genius with anything as sordidly determinate as a poem.

For Adorno, all art contains a utopian moment: 'even in the most sublimated work of art there is a hidden "it should be otherwise" . . . as eminently constructed and produced objects, works of art, including literary ones, point to a practice from which they abstain: the creation of a just life'.[18] By their sheer presence, artefacts testify to the possibility of the non-existent, suspending a debased empirical existence and expressing an unconscious desire to change the world. All art is consequently affirmative – an optimism which is merely the other face of Adorno's political pessimism, and every bit as indiscriminate. Pope's *Essay on Man* must for Adorno be politically progessive, and perhaps more so than *Mother Courage*, since he generally fails to extend to the revolutionary avant-garde the absolution from its sins of content he grants to art in general. Simply by virtue of its forms, art speaks up for the contingent, sensuous and non-identical, bears witness to the rights of the repressed against the compulsive pathology of the identity principle. It redraws the relations between the intellective and the perceptual, and in Kantian vein is similar to the concept without actually becoming one, releasing a mimetic, non-conceptual potential. The artefact tips the balance between subject and object firmly on the side of the latter, ousting the imperialism of reason with a sensuous receptivity to the thing; it thus contains a memory trace of mimesis, of an equable affinity between humanity and nature, which anticipates some future reconciliation between the individual and the collective. As a 'non-regressive integration of divergences', the art work transcends the antagonisms of everyday life without promising to abolish them; it is therefore, perhaps, 'the only remaining medium of truth in an age of incomprehensible terror and suffering'.[19] In it, the hidden irrationality of a rationalized society is brought to light; for art is a 'rational' end in itself, whereas capitalism is irrationally so. Art has a kind of paratactic logicality about it, akin to those dream images which blend cogency and contingency; and it might thus be said to represent an arational reason confronting an irrational rationality. If it acts as an implicit refutation of instrumentalized reason, it is no mere abstract negation of it; rather, it revokes the violence inflicted by such reason by emancipating rationality from its present empirical confinement, and so signifies the process by which rationality criticizes itself without being able to overcome itself.

It would be quite mistaken, however, to imagine that Adorno uncritically affirms modernist culture, setting it over against a dominative society. On the contrary, art is by no means free of the principle of domination, which takes the shape within it of its regulative or constructive drive, that impulse which invests it with a provisional unity and identity. The more the work of art seeks to liberate itself from external determinations, the more it becomes subject to self-positing principles of organization, which mime and internalize the law of an administered society. Ironically, the 'purity' of the modernist work's form is borrowed from the technical, functional forms of a rationalized social order: art holds out against domination in its respect for the sensuous particular, but reveals itself again and again as an ideological ally of such oppression. The 'spiritualization' of the artefact corrects this actual oppressiveness, but is itself secretly modelled on that very structure, assimilating itself to Nature by exerting an unlimited sway over its materials. Art thus releases the specific, but represses it too: 'The ritual of dominating nature lives on in play.'[20] It is not a resolved totality; but it carries within it an impulse to smooth over discontinuities, and all artistic construction thus strains ineluctably towards ideology.

Moreover, if art is subject, like everything else, to the law of objectification, it cannot avoid a kind of fetishism. The transcendence of the artefact lies in its power to dislocate things from their empirical contexts and reconfigurate them in the image of freedom; but this also means that art works 'kill what they objectify, tearing it away from its context of immediacy and real life.'[21] Art's autonomy is a form of reification, reproducing what it resists; there can be no critique without the objectification of spirit, but critique thus lapses to the status of thinghood and so threatens to undo itself. The modernist culture Adorno espouses cannot help positing itself as independent of any conditions of material production, and so insidiously perpetuates false consciousness; but the fetishistic character of the work is also a condition of its truth, since it is its blindness to the material world of which it is a part which enables it to break the spell of the reality principle. If art is always radical, it is also always conservative, reinforcing the illusion of a separate domain of spirit 'whose practical impotence and complicity with the principle of unmitigated disaster are painfully evident.'[22] What it gains in one direction, it loses in another; if it eludes the logic of a degraded history, then it must pay a heavy price for this freedom, part of which is a reluctant reproduction of that very logic.

Art for Adorno is thus less some idealized realm of being than contradiction incarnate. Every artefact works resolutely against itself, and this in a whole variety of ways. It strives for some pure autonomy, but knows that without a heterogeneous moment it would be nothing, vanishing into thin air. It is at once being-for-itself and being-for-society, always simultaneously itself and something else, critically estranged from its history yet incapable of taking up a vantage-point beyond it. By forswearing intervention in the real, artistic reason accrues to itself a certain precious innocence; but at the same time all art resonates with social repression, and becomes culpable precisely because it refused to intervene. Culture is truth and illusion, cognition and false consciousness, at a stroke: like all spirit, it suffers from the narcissistic delusion of existing for itself, but does so in a way which offers to negate all false claims to such self-identity in the commodified world around it. Delusion is art's very mode of existence, which is not to grant it a license to *advocate* delusion. If the content of the art work is an illusion, it is in some sense a necessary one, and so does not lie; art is true to the degree that it is an illusion of the non-illusory. In *positing* itself as an illusion, it exposes the realm of commodities (of which it is one) as unreal, thus forcing illusion into the service of truth. Art is an allegory of undeluded happiness – to which it adds the fatal rider that this cannot be had, continually breaking the promise of the well-being it adumbrates.

In all of these ways, art contains truth and ideology at once. In liberating particulars from the logic of identification, it presents us with an alternative to exchange-value, but thus cons us into the gullible faith that there are things in the world which are not for exchange. As a form of play, it is progressive and repressive at the same time, raising us for a blessed moment above the constraints of practice, but only to draw us back into an infantile ignorance of the instrumental. Artefacts are divided against themselves, at once determinate and indeterminate; and nowhere is this more obvious than in the discrepancy between their mimetic (sensuous-expressive) and rational (constructive-organizational) moments. One of the many paradoxes of art is how the act of making can cause the appearance of a thing unmade; the 'natural' materials which the art work mimes, and the 'rational' form which regulate them, will always be divergent, constituting a slippage or dissonance at the very heart of the work. Mediated through one another, these two dimensions of the artefact are nevertheless non-identical, which allows art's mimetic aspect to provide an implicit criticism of the structuring forms with which it interpenetrates.[23] But this subtle mismatching, which is a question of the work's objective logic, detaches it from the mastery of a singular authorial intention, releases it into autonomy and so permits it to become an image of possible future reconciliation. In a striking irony, it is the art work's inner irreconcilability which puts it at odds with a reified empirical world and thus holds out the promise of a future social harmony. Every work of art pretends to be the totality it can never become; there is never, *pace* Lukács, any achieved mediation of particular and universal, mimetic and rational, but always a diremption between them which the work will cover up as best it can. Artefacts for Adorno are ridden with inconsistencies, pitched battles between sense and spirit, astir with fragments which stubbornly resist incorporation. Their materials will always put up a fight against the dominative rationality which rips them from their original contexts and seeks to synthesize them at the expense of their qualitatively different moments. Complete artistic determination, in which every element of the work would become of equal value, collapses into absolute contingency. The art work is thus centripetal and centrifugal together, a portrait of its own impossibility, living testimony to the fact that dissonance is the truth of harmony.

Such a case, however, is not to be mistaken for the simple-minded hymning of the ineffable particular into which a later, less politically engaged deconstruction has sometimes degenerated. If Adorno is the apologist for difference, heterogeneity and the aporetic, he is also implicated enough in the political struggles of his time to be able to see more than metaphysical delusion in such fundamental human values as solidarity, mutual affinity, peaceableness, fruitful communication, loving kindness – values without which not even the most exploitative social order would succeed in reproducing itself, but which are singularly absent from the disenchanted, post-political discourse of a later, more jejune brand of anti-totalizing thought. Adorno's theory, in other words, holds together in extreme tension positions which in contemporary cultural theory have become ritually antagonistic. Present-day deconstruction is on the whole either silent or negative about the notion of solidarity – a value without which no significant social change is even conceivable, but which deconstruction tends to conflate in Nietzschean fashion with a craven conformity to the law. On the other hand, the work of a Jürgen Habermas might be upbraided for the opposite error, placing too sanguine a trust in a normative collective wisdom. No one could outdo the anti-totalizing animus of a thinker who resoundingly declares that the whole is the false; but Adorno is too deeply dialectical a theorist to imagine that all unity or identity is thus unequivocally terroristic. The given social order is not only a matter of oppressive self-identities; it is also a structure of antagonism, to which a certain notion of identity may be critically opposed. It is because so much post-structuralist thought mistakes a conflictive social system for a monolithic one that it can conceive a consensus or collectivity only as oppressive. Adorno's own case is more nuanced: 'while firmly rejecting the appearance of reconciliation, art none the less holds fast to the idea of reconciliation in an antagonistic world . . . without a perspective on peace art would be untrue, just as untrue as it is when it anticipates a state of reconciliation.'[24] If it is true that 'the urge of the artistic particular to be submerged in the whole reflects the disintegrative death wish of nature',[25] it is also the case that a work of art which dissolved into pure manifoldness would lose 'any sense of what makes the particular really distinctive. Works that are in constant flux and have no unitary point of reference for the many become too homogeneous, too monotonous, too undifferentiated.'[26] Pure difference, in short, is as blank and tedious as pure identity. An art which fails to render its elements *determinate* in their irreconcilability would defuse its critical force; there can be no talk of difference or dissonance without some provisional configuring of the particulars in question, which would otherwise be not dissonant or conflictive but merely incommensurable. 'What we differentiate', Adorno writes in *Negative Dialectics*, 'will appear divergent, dissonant, negative for just as long as the structure of our consciousness obliges it to strive for unity: as long as its demand for totality will be its measure for whatever is not identical with it.'[27] Artefacts are internally unreconciled through a certain reconciliation, which is what leaves them irreconcilable with empirical reality: 'the determined opposition of every art work to empirical reality presupposes its inner coherence.'[28] Unless the work has some kind of fragile, provisional identity, one cannot speak of its resisting political power. Those who indiscriminately demonize such concepts as unity, identity, consensus, regulation have forgotten that there are, after all, different modalities of these things, which are not all equivalently repressive. In Adorno's view, the 'rational' form of art allows for a 'non-repressive synthesis of diverse particulars . . . it preserves them in their diffuse, divergent and contradictory condition.'[29] Non-identity is constitutive of the work of art, but this non-identity 'is opaque only for identity's claims to be total',[30] and pure singularity is sheer abstraction. The general features of the art work emerge from its minute specifications; but this should not be taken to authorize some brusque exorcism of the concept, which would only surrender us to the spell of the brute object. The principle of individuation, Adorno reminds us, has its limits just like any other, and neither it nor its opposite should be ontologized. 'Dadaism, the deictic gesture pointing to pure thisness, was no less universal than the demonstrative pronoun "this".'[31]

Adorno takes from Kant the insight that although the work of art is indeed a kind of totality, it is not one which can be thought along customary conceptual lines. The Kantian aesthetic posits some peculiar imbrication of part and whole, an intimacy which can then be read in two directly contrary ways. Either the whole is no more than the obedient product of the particulars, ceaselessly generated up out of them; or its power is now more pervasive and well-founded than ever, inscribed within each individual element as its informing structure. From this viewpoint, the very attempt to give the slip to a 'bad' totality keels over into its opposite. Kant opens a path towards thinking totality otherwise, but remains caught within a more traditional logic; Adorno presses Kant's privileging of the particular to an extreme limit, insisting on its recalcitrance to whatever force offers to integrate it. The concept of constellation can thus be read as a political rallying cry: 'All power to the particulars!' Yet Adorno's aesthetics incorporates this radical programme of demo-cratic self-government with a more classical dominative model, at times viewing the 'rationality' of the art work as non-repressive, at other times underlining its collusion with bureaucracy. What might undo the 'totalitarian' implications of Kantian aesthetics is the idea of affinity or mimesis – the non-sensuous correspondences between disparate features of the artefact, or more generally the filiations of both kinship and otherness between subject and object, humanity and nature, which might provide an alternative rationality to the instrumental. One might even name this mimesis *allegory*, that figurative mode which relates through difference, preserving the relative autonomy of a set of signifying units while suggesting an affinity with some other range of signifiers. And while this model is not broached by Adorno as explicitly political, it surely carries significant political implications. It would mean, for example, that the relations between class struggle and sexual politics could not be conceived along the lines of some Lukácsian 'expressive totality', but mimetically or allegorically, in a set of correspondences which, like the constellation, take the full measure of otherness and disparity. If such a theory gives no comfort to the symbolic totalizers, it will equally be resisted by those for whom affinity or correspondence can only be imagined as tyrannical 'closure'.

'A liberated mankind', Adorno writes, 'would by no means be a totality.'[32] Unlike many of his statements, this is an impeccably Marxist proposition. For Lukács, totality already exists in principle, but has yet to come into its own. Literary realism prefigures that fortunate day, re-creating each phenomenon in the image of the essence it belies. For Adorno, things are quite the reverse: there is indeed, here and now, a total system which integrates everything relentlessly down, but to emancipate non-identity from its voracious maw would be to transform this miserable situation into some future historical 'constellation', in which rational identity would be constituted by that hiatus within each particular which opens it to the unmasterable otherness of its fellows. Such a political order would be as far from some 'totalitarian' regime as it would be from some random distribution of monads or flux of sheer difference; and in this sense there is the basis for a politics in the work of Adorno, as there is only dubiously in that of some of his theoretical successors. Adorno does not abandon the concept of totality but submits it to a materialist mutation; and this is equivalent to transforming the traditional concept of the aesthetic, turning it against itself by redeeming as far as possible its proto-materialist aspects from its totalizing idealism. This operation is then in its turn a kind of allegory of how the promise of bourgeois Enlightenment – the equitable interrelation of free, autonomous individuals – may be salvaged from the dominative reason which is its contradictory accomplice.

In light of this project, Habermas's cursory judgement that negative dialectics leads to nothing is surely too harsh.[33] Indeed Habermas himself elsewhere applauds Adorno and his colleague Max Horkheimer for the judiciousness with which their critique of reason refuses to darken into an outright renunciation of what the Enlightenment, however vainly, intended by the concept of reason.[34] There are some who would argue that, given what Adorno and Horkheimer had seen that rationality amount to in Nazi Germany, this refusal of renunciation was either foolish or all the more impressive. There are others who would argue that, given what they had seen there of the lethal consequences of abandoning reason, their refusal to do so was entirely understandable. Habermas recognizes that Adorno has no desire to press beyond the uncomfortable impasse of a reason turned back upon itself; he wishes simply to endure in the performative contradiction of a negative dialectics, thus remaining faithful to the echoes of an almost forgotten non-instrumental reason which belongs to prehistory. Like his great exemplar Samuel Beckett, Adorno chooses to be poor but honest; he would prefer to suffer the constraints of the tight theoretical place in which he is stuck rather than betray a more fundamental human suffering by foreclosing upon these painful manoeuvres. What tattered shreds of authenticity can be preserved after Auschwitz consist in staying stubbornly impaled on the horns of an impossible dilemma, conscious that the abandonment of utopia is just as treacherous as the hope of it, that negations of the actual are as indispensable as they are ineffectual, that art is at once precious and worthless. Adorno makes a virtue out of agonized vulnerability, as though that is all honesty can these days mean. As in the work of Paul de Man, authenticity, if it exists at all, lies only in the gesture by which one detaches oneself ironically from all inevitably inauthentic engagements, opening a space between the degraded empirical subject and what would at one time have been the transcendental subject, had the latter not now been wholly undermined by the former.[35] For de Man, an endless self-reflexive irony is now the nearest approach we can make to that classical transcendence, in an age when vertigo must serve as the index of veracity. In the shift from early to late capitalism, the liberal humanist subject has indeed fallen upon hard times, and must now be prepared to sacrifice its truth and identity to its freedom, a disseverance which the Enlightenment would have found unintelligible.

Adorno and de Man share, in fact, an important feature: their overreaction to fascism. To speak of overreacting to such a politics might seem strange, but it is surely possible. Adorno was a victim of fascism; de Man, it would appear, was for a while a sympathizer. Those who argue for some continuity between de Man's earlier and later incarnations are surely right to do so; but the continuity in question is largely negative, a matter of the later de Man's extreme reaction to his earlier involvements. The later de Man, traumatized by the philosophy of transcendental signification, metaphysical groundedness and remorseless totalization with which he had earlier consorted, lapses into a jaded liberal scepticism in some ways close to Adorno's own political pessimism, though without its frail utopian impulse. Both figures would seem afflicted for quite different reasons by a paralysing historical guilt, and would prefer to court impotence, deadlock and failure rather than risk the dogmatism of affirmation. Both positions, moreover, have to some extent always already incorporated their own hopelessness, a move which, among other things, renders them less vulnerable to certain impatient accusations.

In *Minima Moralia*, that bizarre blend of probing insight and patrician grousing, Adorno mourns the disappearance from modern civilization of doors that close 'quietly and discreetly', in one of his tiresome bouts of *haut bourgeois* anti-technological nostalgia: 'What does it mean for the subject that there are no more casement windows to open, but only sliding frames to shove, no gentle latches but turnable handles, no forecourt, no doorstep before the

street, no wall around the garden?'[36] One knows, even
before the eye has travelled to the next sentence, that a
reference to the Nazis will be on its way, which indeed
immediately appears: 'The movements machines demand
of their users already have the violent, hard-hitting,
unresting jerkiness of Fascist maltreatment.' That the man
who could so vigilantly sniff out instances of the banalization
of fascism, from Brecht to Chaplin, should permit himself
this trivializing constellation suggests that we should
evaluate with some circumspection the political responses
of a former victim of fascism. In one sense, nobody could
command more authority and respect; in another sense,
the horror of that experience lingers throughout Adorno's
later work as a distorting as well as illuminating perspective.
Something of the same might be said of Paul de Man,
despite the entirely different nature of his implication in
the Nazi period. His later thought must be examined in
the light of his earlier career in much the same way that
the declarations of a positivist or behaviorist must be
considered in the context of his revulsion from an earlier
evangelicalism.

It is by now widely agreed that Adorno's experience of
fascism led him and other members of the Frankfurt school
to travesty and misrecognize some of the specific power-
structures of liberal capitalism, projecting the minatory
shadow of the former sort of regime upon the quite
different institutions of the latter. Much the same confusion
is inherited by some post-structuralist theory, with its
perilously indiscriminate conflation of widely divergent
orders of power, forms of oppression and modalities of
law. The breathtaking subtlety of Adorno's disquisitions
on art are in inverse proportion to the two-dimensional
crudity of some of his political perceptions. Indeed these
two facets of his thought are closely intertwined, as a
defeatist politics generates a compensatorily rich aesthetics.
Even then, however, it must be remembered that Adorno's

historical pessimism is always tempered by a vision, however ragged and threadbare, of the just society. 'The only philosophy which can be responsibly practised in face of despair', reads the concluding, Benjaminian section of *Minima Moralia*,

> is the attempt to contemplate all things as they would present themselves from the standpoint of redemption. Knowledge has no light but that shed on the world by redemption; all else is reconstruction, mere technique. Perspectives must be fashioned that displace and estrange the world, reveal it to be, with its rifts and crevices, as indigent and distorted as it will appear one day in the messianic light.[37]

There can be no doubt that Adorno believes devoutly in the good society, since how otherwise could he experience the misery of its absence quite so keenly? His despair, then, is always an intricately qualified affair, just as his notorious cultural elitism is severely tempered by the readiness he shows to savage a representative of high culture alongside an avatar of the culture industry.

There are, perhaps, two different Adornos, the one somewhat more defeatist than the other. It is possible to read his work as a retreat from the nightmare of history into the aesthetic, and there is enough in his writings to make this a plausible view. It is the most easily caricatured side of his thought: Beckett and Schoenberg as the solution to world starvation and threatened nuclear destruction. This is the Adorno who deliberately offers as a solution what is clearly part of the problem, the political homeopath who will feed us sickness as cure. This Adorno asks us simply to subsist in the near-intolerable strain of an absurdist, self-imploding thought, a thought before which all hubristic system-builders must humble themselves, and which in its extreme discomfort keeps us loyal at some lofty remove to the characteristic stuff of human history. But there is also the other Adorno who still hopes that we might go through the aesthetic and come out in some unnameable place on the other side, the theorist for whom the aesthetic offers a paradigm, rather than a displacement, of emancipatory political thought.[38]

In *Negative Dialectics*, Adorno speaks out explicitly against any attempt to aestheticize philosophy. 'A philosophy that tried to imitate art, that would turn itself into a work of art, would be expunging itself.'[39] A Schellingian solution, in other words, is not to be pursued: but somewhat later in the volume Adorno is writing in Schopenhauerian vein of philosophy as 'a true sister of music. . . its suspended state is nothing but the expression of its inexpressibility'.[40] As the playful and sensuous, the aesthetic is not, Adorno insists, accidental to philosophy; there is a kind of clownish element about knowing thought's remoteness from its object, yet speaking as though one had that object assuredly in hand, and theory must somehow act out this tragicomic discrepancy, foregrounding its own unfinishedness. As a form of thought whose object must always elude it, there is something a little buffoonish about this monarch of the humanities. But if Adorno wants to aestheticize theory in style and form, he is not prepared to avoid the cognitive, for 'cogency and play are the two poles of philosophy, and [philosophy's] affinity to art does not entitle it to borrow from art, least of all by virtue of the intuitions which barbarians take for the prerogatives of art'.[41] The theoretical concept, however, must not relinquish the sensuous yearning which animates the artistic, even if it tends to negate that yearning. 'Philosophy can neither circumvent such negation nor submit to it. It must strive, by way of the concept, to transcend the concept.'[42]

There can be no question for Adorno of aestheticizing philosophy in the sense of reducing cognition to intuition, since art for him is itself in its peculiar way a form of rationality. Where theory *is* to be aestheticized is in its approach to the particular; art does not exactly oust systematic thought, but furnishes it with a model of sensuous receptivity to the specific. This, however, poses an intriguing problem. For how can philosophy learn from the aesthetic if the whole point of the latter is to be strictly untranslatable into discursive thought? The aesthetic would seem to offer itself as a paradigm for a thought into which it refuses to be translated back. Art shows what philosophy cannot say; but either philosophy will never be able to articulate this, in which case the aesthetic is of dubious relevance to it, or it can learn to express the inexpressible, in which case it may no longer be theory but a form of art. Art would thus seem at once the consummation and the ruin of philosophy – the point to which any authentic thought must asymptotically aspire, yet where it would cease to be in any traditional sense thought at all. On the other hand, the shift from the theoretical to the aesthetic, from a dominative reason to a mimetic one, cannot involve a definitive rupture, since, as we have seen, art itself contains an ineluctable moment of domination. Art's deconstruction of theory is never entirely successful, so that philosophy will live on within its other.

Just as artistic modernism figures the impossibility of art, so Adorno's modernist aesthetic marks the point at which the high aesthetic tradition is pressed to an extreme limit and begins to self-destruct, leaving among its ruins a few cryptic clues as to what might lie beyond it. Yet this undermining of classical aesthetics is achieved from *within* the aesthetic, and owes much to the lineages it throws into crisis. Adorno continues to occupy the high ground of aesthetic theory, rather than descending like Habermas to the more hospitable lowlands of a communicative rationality. He would rather stifle than suffocate, and in whole reaches of his work the air feels too rarefied to sustain much biological growth. He begins neither from the good old things nor the bad new things, to adopt a remark of Brecht's, but from the bad old things, from a history which has been wracked and tormented since its inception. According to *Dialectic of Enlightment*, even Odysseus was a bourgeois individualist, and Adam was no doubt another. The only authentic hope is one wrested from the knowledge that things have been atrocious for a very long time, a hope which risks suppressing that knowledge and so becoming inauthentic. Only by remaining faithful to the past can we prise loose its terrifying grip, and this fidelity is forever likely to paralyse us. It is a problem of how one alleviates and keeps faith with suffering at the same time, since the one is always threatening to undercut the other. If Adorno plies the steel he does so as a wounded surgeon, patient and physician together; and his injuries, as Wittgenstein might have said, are the bruises he has sustained from trying to run his head up against the limits of language. The only cure for our sickness is that it should grow worse – that the wounds inflicted on humanity by its own insanity should be left festering and untended, for without their silent testimony to our historical plight we will forget that a remedy is even necessary and thus escape into innocence. The ragged gap which a predatory reason has driven through our inner nature must be kept open, for it is only in this vacant space that something more creative might just germinate, and what we might stuff it with would only be illusion. Things at the worst, as *Macbeth* reminds us, will either cease or climb up again; and Adorno positions his writing at this undecidable point, prepared to back neither possibility. Like Freud, he knows that individual particulars will never rest content under the law's yoke, that the central tenet of traditional aesthetics is a lie; and this friction between part and whole is the source of both hope and despair, the rending without which nothing can be sole or whole, but which may well succeed in deferring such wholeness to judgement day. The aesthetic, which was once a kind of resolution, is now a scandalous impossibility; and Adorno's most ironic move will be to deploy this very impossibility as a device for renewing the tradition of which it is the last faint gasp. As thought must travel beyond itself, so must the aesthetic transcend itself, emptying itself of its authoritarian urges and offensively affirmative instincts until it leaves behind nothing but a ghostly negative imprint of itself, which is probably the nearest we shall get to truth.

Every generation, Benjamin writes, has been endowed with a *'weak* Messianic power'.[43] The revolutionary historian scans the past for this frail salvific impulse, fanning the sparks of hope still stirring among its ashes. Adorno is cabbalistic enough to decipher the signs of redemption in the most wildly improbable places – in the paranoia of identity-thinking, in the mechanisms of exchange-value, between the elliptical lines of a Beckett or in some sudden jarring of a Schoenberg violin. History is awash with the desire for justice and well-being, clamouring for judgement day, labouring to overthrow itself; it is shot through with weak Messianic powers, if only one learns to search for them in the least obvious places. But there is, of course, always another story. If Adorno can detect the longing for happiness in some bureaucratic edict, he is also depressingly skilful at discerning the rapaciousness which lurks within our most edifying gestures. There can be no truth without ideology, no transcendence without betrayal, no beneficence which is not bought at the cost of another's happiness. If the skein of history is meshed as fine as this, then to tug on any one thread of it is to risk unravelling some rare design in the name of unpicking an obstructive knot. Textuality, with Adorno as with some later theorists, thus becomes a rationale for political inertia; *praxis* is a crude, blundering affair, which could never live up to the exquisite many-sidedness of our theoretical insights. It is remarkable how this Arnoldian doctrine is still alive and well today, occasionally in the most 'radical' of circles.

It is no use, however, telling Adorno that Webern will never do anything for the world economy. He knows it already, better even than us, and is more concerned to rub the ridiculousness of his doctrines in our face than to defend them. In Zen-like fashion, it is only when we have grasped their absurdity that illumination might break upon us. If some later theorists have been able to practise their provocative style even more effectively than Adorno himself, it is largely because they lack his profound sense of political responsibility. Adorno recognized the necessity of that style; but he never failed to meditate on its intolerable privilege too, which is what marks him off from a post-Auschwitz generation. If he ironized and equivocated, it was not with some feckless sub-Nietzschean zest but with a heavy heart. It is ironic in its turn that this nostalgic *haut bourgeois* intellectual, with all his mandarin fastidiousness and remorseless tunnel vision, should join the ranks of Mikhail Bakhtin and Walter Benjamin as one of the three most creative and original cultural theorists that Marxism has yet produced.

NOTES

1 Theodor Adorno, *Negative Dialectics* (London, 1973) p. 35.
2 Ibid., p. 146.
3 Ibid., p. 365.
4 Ibid., p. 320.
5 Theodor Adorno, *Minima Moralia* (London 1974) p. 237.
6 Adorno, *Negative Dialectics*, p. 148.
7 Ibid., p. 149.
8 Ibid., p. 5.
9 Ibid., p. 120.

10 Ibid., p. 23.
11 Ibid., p. 85.
12 Ibid., p. 111.
13 Ibid., pp. 33 and 162.
14 Ibid., p. 47.
15 Ibid., p. 83.
16 See on this point Peter Dews, *Logics of Disintegration* (London, 1987) p. 30.
17 Theodor Adorno, *Aesthetic Theory* (London, 1984) p. 325.
18 Theodor Adorno, 'Commitment', in Ernst Bloch *et al.*, *Aesthetics and Politics* (London, 1977) p. 194.
19 Adorno, *Aesthetic Theory*, p. 27.
20 Ibid., p. 74.
21 Ibid., p. 193.
22 Ibid., p. 333.
23 An excellent account of this topic is given by Peter Osborne, 'Adorno and the Metaphysics of Modernism' (unpublished MS).
24 Adorno, *Aesthetic Theory*, pp. 48 and 366.
25 Ibid., p. 78.
26 Ibid., p. 273.
27 Adorno, *Negative Dialectics*, pp. 5–6.
28 Adorno, *Aesthetic Theory*, p. 225.
29 Ibid., p. 207.
30 Adorno, *Negative Dialectics*, p. 153.
31 Adorno, *Aesthetic Theory*, p. 259.
32 Theodor Adorno, Introduction to *The Positivist Dispute in German Sociology* (London, 1976) p. 12.
33 See Peter Dews (ed.), *Jürgen Habermas: Autonomy and Solidarity* (London, 1986) p. 91.
34 Ibid., pp. 154–5.
35 See Paul de Man, 'The Rhetoric of Temporality', in *Blindness and Insight* (Minneapolis, 1983) p. 214.
36 Adorno, *Minima Moralia*. p. 40.
37 Ibid., p. 247.
38 For a critical account of Adorno's use of the aesthetic as political paradigm, see Albrecht Wellmer, 'Reason, Utopia and the *Dialectic of Enlightenment*', in R. J. Bernstein (ed.), *Habermas and Modernity* (Cambridge, 1985).

39 Adorno, *Negative Dialectics*, p. 15.
40 Ibid., p. 109.
41 Ibid., p. 15.
42 Ibid., p. 15.
43 Walter Benjamin, 'Theses on the Philosophy of History', in H. Arendt (ed.), *Illuminations* (London, 1973) p. 256.

# Criticism, Ideology and Fiction:
## *An Interview with Terry Eagleton*

PAYNE  Much of the most recent work in literary theory
has come out of studies of the nineteenth century,
particularly of the Romantics. I'm thinking of Frye's work
on Blake, Bloom on Shelley, Hartman on Wordsworth,
and others. Yet, you've found a particular centre of interest
in the eighteenth century, at least so it would seem from
your work on *Clarissa* and from the way in which you
make use of the periodical essayists in *The Function of
Criticism*. What is there about the eighteenth century that
has particularly attracted you in your work as a theorist?

EAGLETON  The short answer to that might be just that
it's not the nineteenth or twentieth centuries. Given that
Marxist criticism seems to have concentrated so much on
those periods, I thought it would be interesting to extend
back. There is a kind of practical or institutional reason
for that, I suppose, which is that at Oxford we have to
teach a large range of topics for undergraduate purposes,
so I tend to begin, let's say, in 1700 and move onwards.
It's the old English amateur genteel assumption that a
gentleman can read any of his literature and talk about it
to young people. This has hair-raising problems, but at
least it keeps you stretched. You don't then, as an
undergraduate tutor, get pinned into a period. So I suppose

those eighteenth-century topics have been on my mind for a while. But the prospect of actually extending a Marxist critique back that far hadn't really occurred to me until the last few years. I think that the two books focused on the eighteenth century that you've mentioned were really done for different purposes. I got interested in Richardson, but I also saw Richardson as an opportunity to look at the interrelations of various kinds of critical methods, as a kind of meeting point or convergence, and I think the book was as much about that, about a kind of intervention into contemporary critical debates, trying to show the potential compatibility of various contemporary discourses about literature, as about Richardson himself. *The Function of Criticism* has a different kind of motive. It was really to raise the whole question, by standing as far back as one could without quite falling over the edge, of what the modern critical enterprise was about. I found that to look at the Enlightenment was, in a sense, to estrange one's familiar post-Romantic and even Marxist assumptions about the nature of that prospect. So I think it wasn't so much, in *The Function of Criticism*, a sudden interest in eighteenth-century literature. It was rather a sudden awareness that there were historically other kinds of functions for criticism which had, however partially, however different the political circumstances, once existed. Then the task was to look at criticism from Romanticism onwards to see how it might look different in the light of that different starting point.

PAYNE   You admit in the introduction to *The Rape of Clarissa* that there are certain things, quite understandably, which you find unsympathetic about Richardson, about his personality and about his social and political views. Is there any kind of advantage to you in having a figure or a text to focus on that you're not fully sympathetic with, at least not politically?

EAGLETON  I think, yes, Marxist criticism has perhaps too much practised what has been called the hermeneutics of suspicion. I am a little suspicious now of the hermeneutics of suspicion – not that I don't think that it's still necessary, but I find, for example, with some of my students who are trying to practise a Marxist or feminist criticism, that there's something inevitably rather easier about being negative *vis-à-vis* those canonical works than trying, as it were, to operate a redemptive hermeneutic which might, just about, against the grain, salvage something that could be usable in the present. I think the Richardson book, despite my declared antipathy to aspects of him, was really an attempt at a redemptive hermeneutic, which would follow then in a way from my work on Benjamin, who, I think, did, like Brecht, try to practice hermeneutical redemption. And I think that would reflect a different current in my work, from the rather more stringent, sceptical and suspicious earlier phase of *Criticism and Ideology*. I think there was perhaps a necessary period around about the mid-seventies of a kind of demystificatory criticism, which one felt to be essential when, as it were, the canon was riding high and certain interpretations were going uncriticized. I feel that, at least in the British context, there was a shift of climate in left criticism, possibly datable from the early eighties onwards, where, having done that necessary work, it then became important to see what one could salvage, reconstruct, re-evaluate, recycle. I think the Richardson book belonged to that trend.

PAYNE  Continuing to think about new directions in your work, I notice in comparing your first Shakespeare book, *Shakespeare and Society*, with your most recent book on Shakespeare, a considerable difference in your estimate of *The Tempest*, of Prospero, by extension of Shakespeare himself, which seems to come to rest on what you call the unacceptable view of nature that Shakespeare presents in *The Tempest*. What happened to your thinking about Shakespeare between that first book and this most recent one that has brought about that re-evaluation?

EAGLETON   I suppose the short answer is: all the various contemporary literary theoretical developments, which did indeed happen precisely between those two dates; the first Shakespeare book was in the mid-sixties and then there was this one in the mid-eighties. That was exactly the period when theory took off and when I could then come back to Shakespeare – not, incidentally because I positively wanted to; it was because, as the general editor of that series, I had to step into a breach that nobody else would fill, and look at him in light of those developments. I was struck in my own reading of the two books by that difference, although also by curious similarities. It's sometimes remarkable what consistencies remain in one's work. I found, for example, I always tended to come back to the same plays and to some extent to the same kinds of issues, although looked at later on in a very different theoretical light. As for *The Tempest*, Prospero and the rest, I think the recent book probably suppresses, in the interest of making its particular case about the ideology of nature and the negative aspects of that, a certain, should we say, more ecological reading that could be constructed, and that might result in a qualification of that value judgement. I wasn't, incidentally, in either book, terribly concerned about evaluation. There seemed to be other things to do. I think there's been a lot of very useful recent work, largely in Britain, on the canonical Shakespeare, Shakespeare the institution, but, in a way, my later book was taking that kind of work for granted.

PAYNE   Would it be fair to say that the stance of much contemporary theory, in relationship to certain canonical figures like Shakespeare, is to attempt to know the text, say, of *The Tempest*, in a way in which Shakespeare didn't know it, or to know it better than Shakespeare knew it? To rise above it and be somewhat superior to it?

EAGLETON  Yes, there is a strangely dual response among the reviewers of that recent Shakespeare book. Some of them disliked what they took to be its aloofly superior tone, as though Shakespeare were being given four and a half points on ten for not being a modern. Others, strangely, thought that it smacked of idolatry, too uncritical of Shakespeare's assumed status. I think there is in the latest book a certain provocative appropriation of Shakespeare, and that, to a large extent, I think, was deliberate – was an attempt at a kind of demystifying approach for students who might otherwise find his status intimidating. In other words, there was some point and some pleasure in showing how, as it were, he could be 'knocked off', in the British sense, for those critical purposes, and I think I probably did that with a certain rather excessively provocative elan, though clearly with a serious point behind it. I think when I said in the introduction to the book that it was surprising that somehow Shakespeare had managed to read Marx and Wittgenstein and all the rest of it, this was to claim on the one hand that Shakespeare should be looked at in these modern terms, while on the other hand it was to acknowledge that, in certain senses, he seems to have pre-empted us. So I think that both emphases, demystifying Shakespeare and seeing what we can still learn from him, were really coupled together.

PAYNE  One of the things that's clearly appealing about your theoretical work is its generous eclecticism: psychoanalysis, deconstruction, Marxism, feminism, all seem to cohabit in your books in a way that's, in some sense, very generous and engaging. Has that eclectic theoretical stance that you've taken gotten you into difficulties because of your refusal to take hard lines and keep, for example, Marxism in a position of opposition to deconstruction? Has that been a problem?


EAGLETON   It has. For example, I think I've been criticized just about as much for being critical of post-structuralism as I have for too uncritically imbibing it. Maybe if one sits on a fence, one draws fire from both sides. I think that back in the seventies we used to suffer from a certain fetishism of method; we used to think that we have to get a certain kind of systematic method right, and this would be *the* way of proceeding. I think some of my early work, certainly *Criticism and Ideology*, would fall within that general approach. I would now want to say that, at the level of method, pluralism should reign, because what truly defeats eclecticism is not a consistency of method but a consistency of political goal. I think that is where a Marxist has strongly to refuse eclecticism: a Marxist has to define certain urgent political goals and allow, as it were, those to determine questions of method rather than the other way around. Perhaps we used to think of it as the other way around, and that was a theoreticist rather than a political way of thinking. So I'm happy in one sense to be called a pluralist if that means that there's always more than one emancipatory discourse with which one can work. But I say 'emancipatory discourse' to imply also a criterion of discrimination, and thus, let's be frank about it, of exclusion. I see nothing wrong with closure and exclusion *per se*. That is to say, there will always be certain critical and theoretical discourses which will not be emancipatory, and therefore won't be available for one's work. That's the touchstone of discrimination among methods and discourses: those approaches which seem conducive to one's political goals validate themselves, I think, on that ground.

PAYNE   There has, of course, been considerable criticism of recent theory from within theory itself. I'm thinking of that now-famous essay of Todorov's that appeared in *The Times Literary Supplement* a couple of years ago and of Robert Scholes's *Textual Power*, which was a take-off point for Todorov's concern that theory is in danger, perhaps, of becoming actually anti-humanistic. Are there excesses in contemporary theoretical discourse, do you think, that justify that accusation?

EAGLETON   I think that when theory overshoots practice too far, and I'm not speaking here specifically of literary theory, but theory in a wider sense, then that signals a problem. It signals a problem in practical social reality, and of course it tends to drive theory back onto itself in ways that can be counterproductive: it can mean that theory becomes in some sense autonomous, self-generating. I obviously want to argue as a Marxist that theory is not and should not be self-generating, but should be at the service of certain kinds of practice. At the same time I would want to refuse what is now a fairly standard liberal humanist line, that theory is all right as long as it can directly illuminate texts, that is to say, that theory is some humble handmaiden to the still all-centred and all-privileged literary work. The fact that theory overshoots practice from time to time is, as I say, symptomatic of a problem in practical political reality. We have to understand that in certain historical epochs that's probably inevitable. If one looks at recent political history, that is to say, at the period when theory has taken off, one sees certain kinds of intellectual gain, and one also sees the steady closing down of certain kinds of political option and opportunity. Theory then becomes very ambiguous. It becomes, on the one hand, the place where in some notional way, those practical political options might still be nurtured, might still be kept open. On the other hand, it begins then to substitute itself for those practical options, and that's a point of danger. But that danger is also structural and understandable. It's not simply a lamentable accident that can afflict people who have spent too long reading too much theory. It is, itself, a historical and political matter. And there are, one then has to remind oneself, other political histories in which practice far exceeds theory, and theory struggles behind and has to hobble along to catch up with practice. That can happen too.

PAYNE In your *Function of Criticism* you offer a history of the origins of criticism in the public sphere, in the clubs and coffee-houses of London, and at the end of that book you come to the argument that, perhaps, certain criticism should return to that function by entering the public sphere again. There, of course, have been those – I think of Paul de Man as one whose practice of theory, perhaps both in his style of discourse and in his view of criticism – who think of criticism in the opposite way. Given the difficulty of contemporary critical texts – just the difficulty of reading them – how possible is it for a theorist, especially, to get the kind of access to a non-academic audience that would allow criticism to re-enter the public sphere?

EAGLETON Let me say a word about de Man first of all. I think that one of the negative aspects of de Man's criticism is that there is a real fear of that public world as somehow intrinsically inauthentic. There is, in de Man's writing, a kind of constant struggle for what I might call a negative authenticity, that would define itself simply by the act of distancing itself, ironically, from what is assumed to be a degraded, naturalized, reified public world. I don't share the belief that the public world need be that, and therefore I have a different notion of the nature of critical discourse. The question that you ask is clearly, in a sense, the key question for a radical critic. How is a discourse at once to sustain those kinds of arguments and to be more widely available? In my own work, I've tried to alternate more specialist with more popular writing, ever since the almost simultaneous appearance of *Criticism and Ideology*, which was certainly nobody's idea of an easy read, and the little *Marxism and Literary Criticism*, which was meant to be a popularizing of that case. I am, frankly, scandalized by the apparent indifference, even of radical critics, to the political urgency of the task of popularization. I think it is a political responsibility of such critics to try to engage in that, whatever the institutional difficulties that may involve. One reason that I'm editing my Re-reading Literature series for Blackwell's is not, as some people seem to think, so that we can simply smuggle back the canon, though this time from a radical viewpoint, but because it meets the requirements of bringing theory to bear on the bread-and-butter questions of what gets taught, read, discussed in the classroom. That brings theory nearer the knuckle, and is interestingly less tolerable for the critical establishment, which would now seem apparently willing to allow theory to disport itself in its own ghetto, but is understandably more nervous when it begins to approach the texts which are part of routine academic study.

When one's trying, with what intellectual strength one can muster, to examine and roll back ruling-class ideas, then what results is bound often not to be a popularly available discourse, at least in its immediate form. I think it is a proper task for Marxist intellectuals to engage in that way with issues that are bound to be specialist, complex, often technical. There one's speaking about the class struggle at the level of theory. But I think there's also, for the radical critic, an essentially propagandizing task, which fits much less well with the tenor and emphasis of the current academic esablishment, and which is, to that extent, perhaps more disturbing. It's perhaps only critics who, like myself, have already been able to establish themselves in some acceptable academic terms who can then feel confident enough to engage in that task. I've invited young American critics to contribute to my Blackwell series, people who could have done so extremely well, but simply because of the exigencies of tenure, the pressures of the institution, the fear of what kind of image that might produce of their work, they have regretfully had to decline. So I recognize that there may be a certain privilege involved in being able to perform that task.

PAYNE   In your recent collection of essays, *Against the Grain*, you have a piece on John Bayley. Your selection of his work to critique leads me to wonder whether he in some sense represents the kind of traditional literary study, or liberal humanism, that is, in a sense, in opposition to contemporary theory at Oxford. Is there within your university a resistance to theory, as you see it? Or is there a receptivity to it?

EAGLETON   The Bayley piece, in fact, was meant to be – it appeared originally in *New Left Review* – the first of a series of such pieces which would engage with various significant conservative or liberal humanist critics. It happened that, for various reasons, that series didn't come off. So, standing alone now, it perhaps appears to have a significance which it wasn't quite intended to have. As for Oxford, it is a university in which even the liberal humanists, I would say, are in a minority. Oxford hasn't even had its bourgeois revolution yet, let alone anything more interesting. It hasn't even been hit by F. R. Leavis, let alone Jacques Derrida. The combative polemical and critical tradition in Britain has been much more Cambridge-centred; I was originally at Cambridge myself. But over the past few years here, I've been working with quite a strong, broadly based group in the faculty which, rather cheekily, goes by the name of Oxford English Limited (Limited in the sense of Inc.), which is almost entirely composed of undergraduates and graduates, hardly any senior members, perhaps just one or two sympathetic fellow-travellers, who have been fighting these issues on almost every front, not only on the more obvious fronts of women's studies, cultural studies, the issue of ideas, but actually fighting for and occasionally achieving change in teaching methods or syllabus. I think that what has happened in that period, not only here but elsewhere in Britain, is certainly not any signal victories on the part of radical criticism, but I think a definitive, and, I would hope, irreversible shift of ideological climate. Whereas ten years ago, the right wing thought that if it didn't look too closely at these things they might just scuffle quietly away, there's now a recognition that they're here to stay. There's certainly the recognition that one can't go back beyond or before feminist criticism. I think that's irreversible, and the establishment is faced with the choice of either accommodating these currents or of opposing them. But that, I think, would demand on their part the kind of theoretical resources which I don't think they have. If I were to sum up the situation in Britain on this issue, I'd say that the establishment is in fact increasingly intellectually bankrupt. It has no convincing way I can see, other than appeals to intuition or tradition, to oppose these currents. It remains of course institutionally very powerful: a familiar situation in which the right has the power but not the ideas, and the left has the ideas but not the power. This situation is, of course, inseparable from the unemployment situation, which means that many of the young people with the ideas are simply not getting jobs, and where, in the climate created by Thatcher, to play safe in academic appointments is now endemic. The situation in Britain is then a very interesting one, because we've got beyond the point at which these ideas can be merely ignored or quashed, but not yet to the point of a decisive institutional challenge. I think that we're in some twilight zone between those two moments.

PAYNE   There's a famous aside in Richard Rorty's book, *Philosophy and the Mirror of Nature*, where he says that contemporary literary theory now offers the kind of intellectual excitement to young people that they used to be able to find, perhaps in the last century, in German philosophy or in French philosophy. Do you find that with students? Is it the case that there's almost an instinctive intellectual recognition on their part that theory is where the intellectual juices are flowing?

EAGLETON   Yes, I think that is true. I think that is so even here at Oxford. You have to remember that I teach socially disadvantaged children, that is to say, children who have mostly been to expensive private schools. In many ways this institution, not the most typical of British higher education, has the ability to cream off good students from the system. That is to say, its image and its mythology and its pulling power is such that it can get the best range of students, but then, I think, can give them much less than some of them need, want and expect. That's one reason why they then turn to what in a shorthand way we're calling theory, which of course covers a multitude of sins and issues. Yes, theory does have that sense of excitement, and that can be both negative and positive. It can be superficial glamour, and I take Rorty's comment to suggest that, perhaps, among other things. It can also be what, in a strange way, I imagine the first impact of

Leavisism was at Cambridge. I came in on a later wave there, and in on a sense of excitement not due to glossy packaging and glamour, but to the sense that, once again, criticism was seen to be potentially relevant to other kinds of social concerns. It's been my own hunch that if one looks at the history of criticism, the times when it becomes major are exactly the times when it begins to speak of more than itself. Theory, this enigmatic and mysterious entity, represents now that potential moment for us. It represents the option between trying to move out in ways of broader relevance, or allowing criticism to be shunted into a purely technocratic siding of no essential social relevance. I think that is one of the reasons why students pick it up. I think they pick it up because it is, in a certain sense, unnameable, because there is no adequate academic name as yet for that whole congeries of loosely related discourses which we scoop up under the provisional title of theory. It therefore hasn't the kind of secure and, perhaps, stale identity of longer established discourses, and can thus be used in a variety of directions for a variety of ends.

If one looks at the traditional Western understanding of the intellectual, then, it seems to me to be characterized by at least two distinct qualities. An intellectual is not simply somebody who trades in ideas. I have many colleagues who trade in ideas whom I'd be extremely reluctant to call intellectuals. An intellectual is somebody who trades in ideas by transgressing discursive frontiers, because he or she sees the need to do that. Secondly, an intellectual is somebody who trades in ideas in their vital bearing on a wider political culture. If one takes those two, I think, quite traditional criteria by which the Western intellectual has been defined, then it seems to me that theory is where that project now is, and not literary criticism in its pure or more traditional sense. When students then opt for theory, when teachers opt for theory,

I would like to think they are not simply opting for the more glamorous discourse. They're making what, in the deepest way, I think, is a decision about their identity, a decision about whether in some perhaps indirect sense their work could be of wider human relevance. One of the reasons that I find it possible to work in Britain – this may be of some interest to Americans, and I assure you I have no wish to idealize British society, at least not under its present political regime – is that there is still a sense (it may be partly illusory, but I feel it) in which the working intellectual in Britain is not entirely cut off from the wider society. The intellectual in Britain is, in however partial and limited a way, in a position of mediation with the society as a whole. My feeling is – and this may be purely an outsider's viewpoint, and I stand to be corrected – that if I worked in the States, then I would be saying that my identity belongs almost wholly to a specific academic community or, as they would say in the States, to the profession, a word that almost never passes our lips. So this is, as it were, an existential matter as well as a theoretical one. It's a question of whether one feels, at least in principle, there are wider connections that can be made. Some of the work I do is connected with educational television and with the Open University and increasingly with school teachers, seeing if these rather highbrow ideas make some kind of sense in schools, I mean schools in our sense of the term. And that takes us back to the issue of the public sphere, with a different kind of definition of what intellectual work could be. Theory, I think, poses very sharply that possibility, or, if you like, the choice between theory and traditional criticism poses that possibility.

PAYNE   As you look over the state of the art of theory now, whose work will survive, will be significant in the next thirty or forty years?

EAGLETON  Maybe I can come at that a little indirectly. I
find it now very difficult to step back in a kind of meta-
move and see quite where things are generally at. I can
see that in the period of my own earlier work, from
*Criticism and Ideology* onwards, one was really laying in a
theoretical stock, and there was a great deal of learning
and research and familiarizing with new kinds of language
necessary at that time. From the end of the seventies
onwards, there was a kind of watershed or turning-point
where people began to turn back to the issue of the
institution – where, as it were, having laid in their
theoretical armory, there was now the rather startling
question of what one was going to do with it. Given, of
course, that one of the things one could well do with it
was simply to keep perpetuating the industry. I would
have thought that some bodies of theory will survive
because of their intellectual excitement or power, but I
think that what we're in need of and what we will remember
is the body of theory that will more decisively, more
illuminatingly make a difference in terms of what we do.
For a long time, I think, people like myself have patiently
waited for such currents as deconstruction to cash that
blank cheque they once gave us, in which they assured us
that indeed their enterprise was in a broad sense political,
that indeed, in De.rida's own terms, deconstruction is not,
or at least not primarily, a merely textual operation. I now
begin to be quite frankly sceptical about whether that
particular current will deliver on that particular issue, so
powerful are the pressures which tempt it to become simply
another self-reproducing discourse. I'm interested, in that
respect, in feminist criticism, and have advanced it in my
book on Benjamin as a potential paradigm of criticism,
exactly because it is a form of discourse in some sense
rooted in a wider political movement. If one looks back
at the great periods of twentieth-century criticism, and I'm
thinking not so much of Northrop Frye but, say, of

Benjamin, or perhaps of some of the Soviet avant-garde critics, I think it's clear that what they could do, they could do in large part because they were based in some wider movement. The later Benjamin was possible partly because Bertolt Brecht was possible, and Bertolt Brecht was possible because there was a lively cultural dimension to the German labour movement. Since we lack that wider movement and since theory cannot itself legislate it into being, it's difficult, I think, for us to peer into the future and see what will survive and what won't, because the terms in which we pose that question are now bound to be primarily theoretical rather than political. But those may not be the terms in which survivability happens. Brecht, I suppose, reminded us always to be surprised about what gets recycled and what doesn't, and Benjamin reminded us that one must always patiently collect, because one never knows when something is going to come in handy. Therefore, I think prognostication is difficult precisely because we don't know what it is exactly we might in the future need, and it may well not turn out to be what we currently think is most interesting.

PAYNE   What direction is your work now taking? What lies ahead for you and for your readers?

EAGLETON   Well, I've spent several years trying to stop writing books, but it seems to be unavailing. There's no reliable contrascriptive on the market. One's tempted to think of it rather depressingly as just some genetic instinct that keeps forcing its way out. The straight answer to your question is I'm not sure in what direction I should now go. I think that's not only a personal hesitancy, but belongs to the wider question of where things should now be taken. One direction, I think, to revert to what I said about the Blackwell series, is exactly to take theory back into the routine academic world. But where theory itself should develop I am much less sure about. At the moment, I am becoming increasingly interested in the question of aesthetics; I think one can and must push back before theory to a time when what we had was known as aesthetics. One can once again go back to the eighteenth century, to Shaftesbury, to Hume, to Kant, and try again to look at the prehistory of some of these debates, because people now tend to come in perhaps rather late on the argument. If one looks at questions of aesthetics, of ideology, of political society, these are of course questions that concerned the Enlightenment, concerned the Romantics. I would quite like to take them back there and think forward from that point. However, I'm trying very hard not to do so at the moment, since I have written rather a large number of books recently, and it might be an idea to do something less tedious. I have, in fact, done something else. I have a novel appearing in the autumn which, perhaps, is not accidental in that although I didn't write it for any particular reason other than wanting to write it, it maybe reflects the sense of arriving at a certain kind of crossroads – the fact that it isn't any longer very clear to me which direction one should press things in, and therefore not writing theory or criticism might be one way of coping with that problem.

PAYNE There seems to be a considerable amount – an uncommon amount – of joy and good humour in your books. You even speak about this directly when you talk about your attraction to Benjamin.

EAGLETON There's not much joy in Benjamin.

PAYNE Perhaps comedy rather than joy. You are, though optimistic about society? Are you optimistic about the capacity of a working critic to positively influence the direction not only of social thought but of social action in the West?

EAGLETON   I doubt one would say there was much joy and humour in my writing if one was thinking of *Criticism and Ideology*. I think there is a certain break in my work in that respect, which is due to a whole complex of factors, some of which one could hardly be conscious of. One factor would, I think, be feminism: that is to say, I think that the traditional left, and I would include my own early work within that, has sometimes written with a certain kind of tight-lipped, joyless austerity, which I think is very male, and very much bears the marks of the excessively earnest young male intellectual. Middle-aged male intellectuals like myself have had to go through that, and I don't wish to be too dismissive of it. It has the signal virtue of being unsloppy. But I think that feminism and a number of other influences showed me a way in which one could try to write at once seriously and humorously, in other words, try to deconstruct to some degree the opposition between these moods, deconstruct that most bourgeois of all assumptions that the intellect is deadly serious and unpleasurable, and that pleasure is essentially frivolous and non-intellectual. And that comes down for me to style. I've always been very concerned with writing in the quite narrow sense, with the style and quality of writing, perhaps because like some other critics I'm a creative writer *manqué*. The deconstruction of humour and seriousness for me now comes down to a matter of finding a particular way of writing that can be at once committed and, one hopes, more companionable than the somewhat alienated rigours of certain traditional male Marxist discourse. The other influence, I suppose, is that I am of Irish provenance, and the Irish, of course, have always preserved a tradition of wit and humour – largely, I may add, because they've had very little else. Hence the notable darkness and bitterness of much of that humour. I would like to think that my own writing has increasingly been able to unrepress that element in myself. You have to remember that we're speaking here in the British Isles, in part of which a civil war is going on. I'm trying in my own way to rediscover something of my cultural and political heritage. There is always an element of sentimentalism and nostalgia concerned in that, not least, God knows, where the Irish are concerned, but then one shouldn't perhaps be too earnest in dismissing sentiment either. I have for a long time written satirical and political ballads, and indeed, performed them. Perhaps when I first began to write 'serious criticism', I never really saw a way of hooking that up with such more popular kinds of cultural activity. I would hope that, now, there's in my writing an attempt at a greater convergence between the two. And the same really applies to my novel: I was delighted when somebody said that what they liked about it was that, although it was an intellectual novel, it was not an academic novel. As you know, we English critics are rather prone to write academic novels, and, of course, there is quite a difference between writing an academic and an intellectual novel. So, once again, to try to write, as they say, creatively, but also intellectually, would be a desirable stylistic and political goal. I am horrified by the dearth of ideas in contemporary English fiction, which I think has its roots in a certain ingrown English empiricism and commonsensicality, and I think that if there is to be a viable fiction of the left, as well as a theory, then it has to find ways of bringing creative and intellectual discourses together.

# Terry Eagleton: *Selected Bibliography, 1966–1987*

## 1966

1 (Ed.), *Directions: Pointers for the Post-conciliar Church* (London: Sheed and Ward) viii, 214pp.
2 *The New Left Church* (London: Sheed and Ward) x, 180pp.

## 1967

3 (Ed. with Brian Wicker), *From Culture to Revolution* (Cambridge: Slant, The Slant Symposium 1967).
4 *Shakespeare and Society: Critical Studies in Shakespearean Drama* (London: Chatto and Windus; New York: Schocken) 208pp.
5 'Language and Reality in *Twelfth Night*', *Critical Quarterly*, vol. 9, pp. 217–28.

## 1970

6 *The Body as Language* (London: Sheed and Ward) x, 115pp.
7 *Exiles and Émigrés: Studies in Modern Literature* (London: Chatto and Windus) 227pp.

## 1971

8 'History and Myth in Yeats's "Easter 1916" ', *Essays in Criticism*, vol. 21, pp. 248–60.
9 'Thomas Hardy: Nature as Language', *Critical Quarterly*, vol. 13, pp. 155–62.

## 1972

10 'Class, Power and Charlotte Brontë', *Critical Quarterly*, vol. 14, pp. 225–35.

## 1973

11 'Nature and the Fall in Hopkins: A Reading of "God's Grandeur" ', *Essays in Criticism*, vol. 23, pp. 68–75.

## 1975

12 'The Poetry of Peter Dale', *Agenda*, vol. 13, no. 3, pp. 85–91.

## 1976

13 *Criticism and Ideology: A Study in Marxist Literary Theory* (London: New Left Books; Atlantic Highlands, NJ: Humanities Press) 191pp.
14 *Marxism and Literary Criticism* (London: Methuen; Berkeley: University of California Press) 87pp.
15 *Myths of Power: A Marxist Study of the Brontës* (London: Macmillan) 148pp. Second edition, 1988, xix, 148pp.
16 'Sylvia's Lovers and Legality', *Essays in Criticism*, vol. 26, pp. 17–27.

## 1977

17 'Marxist Literary Criticism', in Schiff, Hilda (ed.), *Contemporary Approaches to English Studies* (London: Heinemann) pp. 94–103. Reprinted in *Sociological Review*, Monograph M25 (Wadham College, Oxford) pp. 85–91.
18 'Raymond Williams e il populismo', *Calibano*, vol. 1, pp. 159–84.

## 1978

19 'Form, Ideology, and *The Secret Agent*', *Sociological Review*, Monograph M26 (Wadham College, Oxford,) pp. 55–63. Reprinted in *Against the Grain* (1986).

## 1979

20 'The Poetry of E. P. Thompson', *Literature and History*, vol. 5, pp. 139–45.
21 'Radical Orthodoxies', *Oxford Literary Review*, vol. 3, no. 3, pp. 99–103.
22 Review of *Modes of Modern Writing* by D. Lodge, *Literature and History*, vol. 5, pp. 232–3.
23 Review of *Solitude in Society: Sociological Study in French Literature* by R. Sayre, *Literature and History*, vol. 5, p. 269.

## 1980

24 'Text, Ideology, Realism', in Said, Edward W. (ed.), *Literature and Society* (Baltimore: Johns Hopkins University Press) pp. 149–73.
25 Review of *Fictions and Ceremonies* by D. Chaney, *Literature and History*, vol. 6, pp. 255–6.
26 Review of *Field Work* by S. Heaney, *Forced March* by M. Radnoti, *Moortown* by T. Hughes, *Poets from the North of*

*Ireland* by F. Ormsby, and *Selected Poems 1950–1975* by T. Gunn, *Stand Magazine*, vol. 21, no. 3, pp. 76–80.

27 Review of *Ideology and Cultural Production* by M. Barrett, P. Corrigan, A. Kuhn and J. Wolff, *Literature and History*, vol. 6, no. 2, pp. 255–6.

28 Review of *Tropics of Discourse: Essays in Cultural History* by H. White, *Notes and Queries*, vol. 27, no. 5, p. 478.

29 Review of *Political Fictions* by M. Wilding, *Meanjin*, vol. 39, no. 3, pp. 383–8.

30 Review of *Semiotics of Poetry* by M. Riffaterre and *Textual Strategies: Perspectives in Post-Structuralist Criticism* by J. V. Harari, *Literature and History*, vol. 6, no. 2, pp. 256–7.

31 Review of *Socialist Propaganda in the 20th-Century British Novel* by D. Smith, *Review of English Studies*, vol. 31, pp. 106–7.

32 Review of *Tragic Realism and Modern Society* by D. Orr, *Literature and History*, vol. 6, no. 1, pp. 117–18.

## 1981

33 *Walter Benjamin, or Towards a Revolutionary Criticism* (London: New Left Books) 187pp.

34 'The End of Criticism', *Southern Review (Adelaide)*, vol. 14, no. 2, pp. 99–106.

35 'The Idealism of American Criticism', *New Left Review*, no. 127, pp. 53–65. Also as 'El idealismo de la critica norteamericana', *Escritura: Revista de Teoria y Critica Literarias* (Caracas), vol. 6, no. 12, pp. 247–61. Reprinted in *Against the Grain* (1986).

36 'Marxism and Deconstruction', *Contemporary Literature*, vol. 22, no. 4, pp. 477–88.

37 'Psychoanalysis, the Kabbala and the Seventeenth Century' in Barker, Francis, *et al.* (eds), *1642: Literature and Power in the Seventeenth Century* (Colchester: Department of Literature, University of Essex) pp. 201–6.

38 Review of *Carminalenia* by C. Middleton, *Decadal: 10 Years of Sceptre Press* by M. Booth, *Gravities* by S. Heaney and N. Connor, *The Sea of Fire* by R. Brennan, *Selected Poems*

by P. Beer, *The Traveler Hears the Strange Machine* by D. Stanford, and *A Watching Brief* by R. McFadden, *Stand Magazine*, vol. 22, no. 2, pp. 73–7.

39 Review of *The Collected Ewart, 1933–1980, Extractions*, by C. H. Sisson, *The Man I Killed* by L. Lerner, *New Collected Poems* by V. Scannell, *Poems of Love and Death* by G. Macbeth, *Stand Magazine*, vol. 22, no. 4, pp. 74–8.

40 Review of *Critical Assumptions* by K. K. Ruthven and *Narrative and Structure: Exploratory Essays* by J. Holloway, *Review of English Studies*, vol. 32, pp. 498–9.

41 Review of *Interpretation: An Essay in the Philosophy of Literary Criticism* by P. D. Juhl, *Literature and History*, vol. 7, no. 2, pp. 242–4.

42 Review of *One-dimensional Marxism: Althusser and the Politics of Culture* by S. Clarke, T. Lovell, K. McDonnell, K. Robins and V. Jeleniewskiseidler, *French Studies*, vol. 35, no. 3, pp. 369–70.

43 Review of *Working with Structuralism* by D. Lodge, *New Society*, vol. 56, pp. 535–6.


## 1982


44 *The Rape of Clarissa: Writing, Sexuality, and Class-Struggle in Samuel Richardson* (Oxford: Basil Blackwell). 109pp.

45 'Fredric Jameson: The Politics of Style', *Diacritics*, vol. 12, no. 3, pp. 14–22. Reprinted in *Against the Graint* (1986).

46 'Macherey and Marxist Literary Theory', in Parkinson, G. H. R. (ed.), *Marx and Marxisms* (Cambridge: Cambridge University Press) pp. 145–55. Reprinted in *Against the Grain* (1986).

47 'The Revolt of the Reader', *New Literary History*, vol. 13, no. 3, pp. 449–52. Reprinted in *Against the Grain* (1986).

48 'Terry Eagleton', an interview with James H. Kavanagh and Thomas E. Lewis, *Diacritics*, vol. 12, no. 1, pp. 53–64.

49 'Wittgenstein's Friends', *New Left Review*, no. 135, pp. 64–90. Reprinted in *Against the Grain* (1986).

50 Review of *After the Dream* by A. Rudolf, *Collected Poems* by J. K. Baxter, *Danta Gradha* by A. Young, *English*

*Subtitles* by P. Porter, *The Flood* by C. Tomlinson, *Poems 1913–1956 by Bertolt Brecht*, ed. J. Willett and R. Manheim, *Sea to the West* by N. Nicholson, *Tree* by R. Burns and *XXI Poems* by G. Squires, *Stand Magazine*, vol. 23, no. 2, pp. 62–8.

51 Review of *The Book of Jupiter* by T. Paulin and N. Connor, *The Butchers of Hull* by P. Didsbury, *Fox Running* by K. Smith, *The Go Situation* by M. Foley, *Night Cries* by J. Cassidy, *A Rumoured City – New Poets from Hull* by D. Dunn, *The Sorrow Garden* by T. McCarthy and *The Younger Irish Poets* by G. Dawe, *Stand Magazine*, vol. 24, no. 2, pp. 66–72.

52 Review of *The Fortunate Traveller* by D. Walcott, *Out of the Elements* by A. Waterman, *The Selected John Hewitt*, ed. A. Warner, *An Unofficial Rilke* by M. Hamburger and *Variations* by M. Hamburger, *Stand Magazine*, vol. 24, no. 1, pp. 68–72.

53 Review of *Romanticism and Ideology* by D. Aers, J. Cook and D. Punter and *The Social Function of Art* by J. Wolff, *Literature and History*, vol. 8, no. 2, pp. 255–6.

54 Review of *The Sociology of Art* by A. Hauser, *The Times Literary Supplement*, no. 4151, p. 1168.

55 Review of *Writers of Wales: Raymond Williams* by J.P. Ward, *Poetry Wales*, vol. 17, no. 4, pp. 87–9.

## 1983

56 *Literary Theory: An Introduction* (Oxford: Basil Blackwell; Minneapolis: University of Minnesota Press) vii, 244 pp.

57 'The Task of the Cultural Critic (Politics and Culture)', *Meanjin*, vol. 42, no. 4, pp. 445–8.

58 (With D. Bleich, *et al.*), 'Literary Theory in the University – A Survey', *New Literary History*, vol. 14, no. 2, pp. 411–51.

59 'Power and Knowledge in "The Lifted Veil" ', *Literature and History*, vol. 9, no. 1, pp. 52–61.

60 (With P. Fuller), 'The Question of Value – A Discussion', *New Left Review*, no. 142, pp. 76–90.

61  Review of *Beautiful Theories: The Spectacle of Discourse in Contemporary Criticism* by E. W. Bruss, *The Times Literary Supplement*, no. 4182, p. 546.

62  Review of *The Cornish Dancer* by G. Grigson, *The Flower Master* by M. McGuckian, *New and Selected Poems* by A. Cronin, *The Occasions of Poetry* by T. Gunn, *Selected Poems* by J. Montague and *The Sunflower of Hope – Poems from the Mozambican Revolution* by C. Searle, *Stand Magazine*, vol. 24, no. 3, pp. 77–80.

63  Review of *Deconstruction – Theory and Practice* by C. Norris and *Inventions: Writing, Textuality and Understanding in Literary History* by G. L. Burns, *Literature and History*, vol. 9, no. 2, pp. 260–2.

64  Review of *Devotions* by C. Wilmer, *The Hunt by Night* by D. Mahon, *A Late Harvest* by J. Ward, *Making Arangements* by M. Simpson, *A Second Life* by W. Scammell and *The Selected Paul Durcan*, ed. E. Longley, *Stand Magazine*, vol. 25, no. 1, pp. 77–80.

65  Review of *The Institution of Criticism* by P. U. Hohendahl, *Literature and History*, vol. 9, no. 1, pp. 97–101.


**1984**

66  *The Function of Criticism: From the Spectator to Post-Structuralism* (London and New York: Verso) 133pp.

67  'Nature and Violence: The Prefaces of Edward Bond', *Critical Quarterly*, vol. 26, nos 1–2, pp. 127–35.

68  'The Rise of English Studies: An Interview with Terry Eagleton', *Southern Review* (Adelaide), vol. 17, no. 1, pp. 18–32.

69  (With Tony Bennett, Noel King, Ian Hunter, Catherine Belsey and John Frow), 'The "Text in Itself": A Symposium', *Southern Review* (Adelaide), vol. 17, no. 2, pp. 115–46.

70  Review of *W. H. Auden – The Critical Heritage* by J. Haffenden and *Auden – A Carnival of Intellect* by E. Callan, *Poetry Review*, vol. 73, no. 4, pp. 60–1.

71  Review of *Black Literature and Theory*, ed. H. L. Gates, *New York Times Book Review*, vol. 8, p. 45.

72 Review of *Collected Poems 1941–1983* by M. Hamburger and *Poems and Epigraphs* by J. M. v. Goethe, ed. M. Hamburger, *The Times Literary Supplement*, no. 4230, p. 454.

73 Review of *Human Rites – Selected Poems 1970–1982* by E. A. Markham and *Midsummer* by D. Walcott, *The Times Literary Supplement*, no. 4258, p. 1290.

74 Review of *Interrelations of Literature* by J. P. Barricelli and J. Gibaldi and *Literary Criticism and the Structures of History: Eric Auerbach and Leo Spitzer* by G. Green, *Modern Language Review*, vol. 79, no. 8, pp. 385–6.

75 Review of *Inviolable Voice – History and 20th-Century Poetry* by S. Smith, *Stand Magazine*, vol. 25, no. 2, pp. 47–9.

76 Review of *Liberty Tree* by T. Paulin, *111 Poems* by C. Middleton, *Quoof* by P. Muldoon, *A Round House* by M. Sweeney and *Selected Poems* by F. Adcock, *Stand Magazine*, vol. 25, no. 3, pp. 76–80.

77 Review of *Marxism and Modernism – An Historical Study of Lukács, Brecht, Benjamin and Adorno* by E. Lunn, *Journal of Modern History*, vol. 56, no. 1, pp. 124–5.

78 Review of *Modern French Marxism* by M. Kelly, *French Studies*, vol. 38, no. 1, p. 112.

79 Review of *News for Babylon – The Chatto Book of West Indian–British Poetry* by J. Berry, *Poetry Review*, vol. 74, no. 2, pp. 57–9.

80 Review of *Poetry and the Sociological Idea* by J. P. Ward, *Review of English Studies*, vol. 35, no. 139, pp. 427–8.

81 Review of *Sex and Enlightenment: Women in Richardson and Diderot* by R. Goldberg, *The Times Literary Supplement*, no. 4254, p. 1170.

82 Review of *Sexuality in 18th-Century Britain* by P. G. Bouce, *Notes and Queries*, vol. 31, no. 1, pp.129–30.

## 1985

83 (Ed. with prefaces to each volume), *Rereading Literature* (Oxford: Basil Blackwell, 1985– ). Volumes published to date: *W. H. Auden* by Stan Smith (1985), *William Blake* by

Edward Larrissy (1985), *Emily Brontë* by James H. Kavanagh (1985), *Charles Dickens* by Steven Connor (1985), *Alexander Pope* by Laura Brown (1985), *Geoffrey Chaucer* by Stephen Knight (1986), *William Shakespeare* by Terry Eagleton (1986), *Alfred Tennyson* by Alan Sinfield (1986), *Ben Jonson* by Peter Womack (1987), *Virginia Woolf* by Rachel Bowlby (1988), *John Milton* by Catherine Belsey (1988) and *Thomas Hardy* by John Goode (1988).

84  'Brecht and Rhetoric', *New Literary History*, vol. 16, no. 3, pp. 633–8. Reprinted in *Against the Grain* (1986).

85  'Capitalism, Modernism, and Post-Modernism', *New Left Review*, no. 152, pp. 60–73. Reprinted in *Against the Grain* (1986).

86  'Ideology and Scholarship', in McGann, Jerome J. (ed.) *Historical Studies and Literary Criticism* (Madison: University of Wisconsin Press) pp. 114–25.

87  (With Patrice Petro and Andrew Martin), 'Interview with Terry Eagleton', *Iowa Journal of Literary Studies*, vol. 6, pp. 1–17.

88  'Literature and History', *Critical Quarterly*, vol. 27, no. 4, pp. 23–6.

89  'Marxism and the Past', *Salmagundi*, vol. 68, no. 6, pp. 271–90.

90  'Marxism, Structuralism, and Post-Structuralism', *Diacritics*, vol. 15, no. 4, pp. 2–12. Reprinted in *Against the Grain* (1986).

91  'Politics and Sexuality in W. B. Yeats', *Crane Bag*, vol. 9, no. 2, pp. 138–42.

92  'New Poetry', *Stand Magazine*, vol. 26, no. 1, pp. 68–72.

93  Review of *By the Fisheries* by J. Reed, *Caribbean Poetry Now* by S. Brown, *Collected Poems* by C. H. Sisson, *The Dead Kingdom* by J. Montague and *Shadow Lands* by J. Bobrowski, *Stand Magazine*, vol. 26, no. 2, pp. 66–70.

94  Review of *Collected Poems*, vol. 1, by M. Hartnett, *From The Irish* by J. Simmons, *The Price of Stone* by R. Murphy and *The Rhetorical Town* by S. Barry, *Poetry Review*, vol. 75, no. 2, pp. 64–5.

95  Review of *Dark Glasses* by B. Morrison, *Minding Ruth* by A. C. Mathews, *The Non-aligned Storyteller* by T. McCarthy,

*Poems 1963–1983* by H. Longley and *Rich* by C. Raine, *Stand Magazine*, vol. 26, no. 4, pp. 69–72.

96 Review of *The Literary Labyrinth* by B. Sharratt, *Poetics Today*, vol. 6, no. 4, pp. 780–2.

97 Review of *Reading for the Plot* by P. Brooks, *Literature and History*, vol. 11, no. 2, pp. 295–6.

98 Review of *The Rise and Fall of Structural Marxism: Althusser and His Influence* by T. Benton, *French Studies*, vol. 39, no. 2, pp. 239–40.


**1986**


99 *Against the Grain: Essays 1975–1985* (London and New York: Verso) 199 pp. Includes 'Macherey and Marxist Literary Theory', 'Form, Ideology and *The Secret Agent*', 'Liberality and Order: The Criticism of John Bayley', 'The Idealism of American Criticism', 'Fredric Jameson: The Politics of Style', 'Frère Jacques: The Politics of Deconstruction', 'Marxism, Structuralism and Post-structuralism', 'Wittgenstein's Friends', 'Capitalism, Modernism and Postmodernism', 'The Critic as Clown', 'Brecht and Rhetoric', 'Poetry, Pleasure and Politics', 'The Revolt of the Reader' and 'The Ballad of English Literature'.

100 *William Shakespeare* (Oxford and New York: Basil Blackwell) 114pp., 'Re-reading Literature' series.

101 'The Poetry of Radical Republicanism', *New Left Review*, no. 158, pp. 123–8.

102 'Political Criticism' in Caws, Mary Ann (ed.), *Textual Analysis: Some Readers Reading* (New York: Modern Language Association) pp. 257–71.

103 Review of *L'Aventure Semiologique* by R. Barthes and *The Responsibility of Forms: Critical Essays on Music, Art, and Representation* by R. Barthes, *The Times Literary Supplement*, no. 4335, p. 477.

104 Review of *The Definition of Literature and Other Essays* by W. W. Robson, *Modern Language Review*, vol. 81, p. 428.

105 Review of *Collected Poems* by D. Egan, *Family Matters* by E. A. Markham, *The Fat Black Woman's Poems* by G.

Nichols, *Long Road to Nowhere* by A. Johnson, *Third World Poems* by E. K. Braithwaite and *Trio 4* by A. Elliott, L. McAuley and C. O'Driscoll, *Stand Magazine*, vol. 27, no. 4, pp. 76–9.

106 Review of *Freud and the Culture of Psychoanalysis* by S. Marcus, *History Workshop: A Journal of Socialist and Feminist Historians*, vol. 22, pp. 193–4.

107 Review of *A Reader's Guide to Contemporary Literary Theory* by R. Selden, *Modern Language Review*, vol. 81, pp. 959–60.

108 Review of *Reading Althusser: An Essay on Structural Marxism* by S. G. Smith, *Journal of Modern History*, vol. 58, no. 1, 258–9.

109. Review of *V* by T. Harrison, *Poetry Review*, vol. 76, nos 1–2, pp. 20–2.


## 1987

110 *Saints and Scholars* (London and New York: Verso) 145pp.

111 'The End of English', *Textual Practice*, vol. 1, no. 1, pp. 1–9.

112 'Estrangement and Irony in the Fiction of Milan Kundera', *Salmagundi*, vol. 73, pp. 25–32.

113 'Frère Jacques: The Politics of Deconstruction', *Semiotica*, vol. 63, pp. 3–4.

114 Review of *A Furnace* by R. Fisher, *The Lame Waltzer* by M. Sweeney, *A New Primer for Irish Schools* by D. Bolger and M. O'Loughlin, *Letter to an Englishman* by A. Cronin, *A Northern Spring* by F. Ormsby and *Standing Female Nude* by C. K. Duffy, *Stand Magazine*, vol. 28, no. 2, pp. 68–72.

115 Review of *Cuts* by M. Bradbury and *No, Not Bloomsbury* by M. Bradbury, *The Times Literary Supplement*, no. 4393, p. 627.

116 Review of *Fragments of Modernity* by D. Frisby, *Sociological Review*, vol. 35, no. 1, pp. 178–80.

117 Review of *Theories of Discourse: An Introduction* by D. MacDonell, *Literature and History*, vol. 13, no. 1, pp. 137–8.

# Index